SIRATA

INNER AND OUTER JOURNEYS

The wound is the place where the Light enters you. **Rumi**

Songlines

This book follows our personal songlines, our journey that allowed us to mysteriously unravel the unchartered territories of our souls. Australian Aborigines walk along invisible routes, called songlines or dreaming tracks across the land or sometimes the sky, which link the member of a clan to important sites. These indigenous memory codes offer rich explanations about country, the traditions and the sense of connection. We are writing this book while living in the south of Perth and would like to pay our respects to the Traditional Custodians, the Noongar people.

We, Majnun and Leyla, have been soulmates for over twenty-five years. Our relationship is the vessel that has made our transformations possible. While we each discover our own individual songlines, we benefit greatly from their intersecting points that at times left us questioning whether to turn left or right. Walking the unknown territory of a relationship and challenges life tends to confront you with have left us on our knees at times praying for a divine compass.

I, Majnun, am Australian-born, a former Christian Brother, which is an order for men within the Catholic Church, an educator and a counselling therapist. I began to follow the Sufi path after I met Leyla. As you'll discover in this book, I have experienced quite profound trauma and abuse, which I didn't begin to recognise until I was past the age of 60. Childhood abuse made it difficult at times to connect with my true self. In this book, we describe the process that helped me reconnect to my essential nature and put my fragmented soul back together. Through my journey with Leyla, I have come to accept my past and move beyond it. My abuse is no longer a secret, life-limiting event.

I, Leyla, am a university lecturer with a PhD in Education (1996) and second PhD in Spiritual Anthropology (2016). I have been following the Sufi path for over 30 years. I have always been a free spirit with a love for languages, literature and travelling. My greatest pleasure is to get in the car, not knowing where I will end up. As you will see, this open-ended adventurous spirit is not limited to car journeys. The inner songlines we have followed individually and as a couple have required a total acceptance of open-ended unknowingness. I have supported Majnun through every step of his recovery. When we first met, I had no idea about his past traumatic experiences. How could I? He was always polite, kind and easy going.

We have travelled together on a long, at times difficult journey of discovery and psychological and spiritual healing. We've now reached a place of ongoing curiosity based on peaceful surrender. In this book, we recount our inner and outer trajectories so far in the hope that they will encourage and support others.

Since we met, we've lived a spiritual journey together – of study, prayer, inquiry and faith. Both of us are committed to the Sufi path and we spent several years studying the teachings of the Diamond Approach. In addition, we practise a process of inquiry that helps us to look deeply into current issues and hold the tension until we find direction. This has taught us to trust our inner wisdom and seek guidance, rather than rely solely on our logical and rational minds.

The beauty of moving along spiritual songlines is that they never end. We put our faith in God, each other and in our daily practice of Sufism. Most of this book is told in our own words, as our personal stories, interspersed with commentary and some of Leyla's writings.

The meeting of two personalities is like the contact of two chemical substances: if there is any reaction, both are transformed. Carl Jung

Beginnings – Majnun

Leyla and I met in 1994, at a weekend retreat in Sydney organised by the Diamond Approach. I was new to the Diamond Approach, but Leyla had been studying it for some time by then.

Because a close friend suggested that I would enjoy it, I went along as I was keen to learn about all sorts of different spiritual paths. At that time, I was a counsellor, working from my home in Sydney in my own private practice. It was a few months after I'd left the Christian Brothers, so I was still adjusting to my new life.

I first noticed Leyla because she appeared to have a deep understanding of the teachings of the Diamond Approach. After the teacher had covered the relevant material for the day, Leyla would often spend time with some of the participants to help us translate the theory into practical application.

Because I'd studied the depth psychological traditions as part of my Master's Degree in psychology, the Diamond Approach teachings resonated very strongly in me. I sensed that Leyla could access her inner life and her unconscious more easily than many other people, which gave her a profound understanding of the teachings.

Over time we became good friends through attending the Diamond Approach retreats, and I started to trust her. We talked a lot about the input, and I learned a lot from Leyla's insights. As time passed, it was increasingly clear there was a chemistry between us.

After we'd known each other for about two years, I had a deeply moving dream about us. It was surprising for me to have such a vivid dream about a place I'd never been and an occasion I'd never thought about. I dreamt we were on our honeymoon, in a little village in the Mediterranean with white cottages and boats on the harbour. The next time we talked on the phone, I shared it with her, and it was the catalyst for our relationship developing into something more. Dreams and visions are a very important part of the Sufi and Jungian traditions, and I knew Leyla would see the dream as important.

Early in our friendship, I also had a strong vision of Leyla as a powerful black horse that wants to be free and must not be constrained by a fence. The vision helped me understand that Leyla needs a lot of freedom. She's powerful and knowledgeable and can't be constrained by people or circumstances. I knew right from the beginning that if our relationship was to work, I mustn't try to restrict Leyla's sense of adventure.

Not long after our phone conversation about my dream, we agreed to meet at a suburban railway station in Sydney and visit Leyla's brother Guido together. What we didn't agree on was where exactly to meet at the station, and this was in the days before mobile phones. The station has two subway exits, on different sides of the track. It was like a movie script: I was waiting on one side, and Leyla was waiting on the other. Neither of us knew the other was there. I waited for about 15 minutes, wondering whether Leyla had decided not to turn up. I hadn't seen her since I'd told her about the dream, and I thought this was the turning point in our relationship. I felt there was a real risk she'd decided not to come.

Eventually, I decided to walk back down the ramp and check inside the station itself. At exactly the moment, Leyla made the same decision on the other side of the station. We met in the middle, and it was the moment we both knew for sure that we were meant to be together. That was our first kiss. It was as though we were so in tune with each other that we knew the exact instant to walk back through the subway and meet.

What ails thee? – Majnun

For most of my life, I have felt there was something fundamentally wrong with me, but I didn't know what it was. I had a deep, internal belief that something was amiss – that I had done something bad and that there was something profoundly flawed with me as a person. I felt a pervasive sense of shame.

This feeling of inadequacy was a big contributing factor to my anxiety. I've always been anxious. I can't remember being any other way. Every morning when I wake up, I feel anxious about the day ahead. In the past few years my anxiety has begun to reduce. It's not as overwhelming and debilitating as it used to be, but it's still there in the background.

The odd thing about anxiety is that other people don't necessarily notice it. When I was a child, people thought I was placid and shy. In my work now, people think I'm calm and confident. Thankfully, I've developed a calm exterior that allows me to keep functioning. People see my good manners and thoughtful approach, and they think I'm calm. But in reality, underneath, I feel anxious every day.

When I was about ten years old, in Year 5 at school, I used to walk past a monastery that belonged to an order of priests. It was a place where priests lived, not a parish church, and it had a chapel attached to it. I started going into the chapel to go to confession because I was convinced, I had committed a sexual mortal sin, and I wanted to confess it and be forgiven. I was just a ten- year-old boy, and I didn't even know what my mortal sin was. But every time I went into the confession box, I insisted I was guilty of having done something terrible. However, I could never say any more than that. I couldn't name what had happened or what was wrong.

The priests there were enormously patient with me. They listened to my confessions and asked questions about what had happened. They always told me I was forgiven. But every time I left the confession box, I felt dissatisfied because I knew I hadn't been able to name what exactly I had done wrong or what had happened. Given that I had no internal access to what I felt was a mortal sin, I was convinced that I couldn't be forgiven. I carried a sense of deep shame and was left with unresolved guilt.

By the time I reached high school, my conviction that something was wrong with me was strong enough to stop me from doing things other teenage boys did. My lack of confidence resulted in me doing everything possible to disappear within my class. I didn't volunteer to do anything or try out for new things because I didn't want to be noticed and therefore remained quiet and withdrawn most of the time.

The Christian Brothers school that I attended required me to join the military cadets – either the army or the air force cadets. I chose the army cadets. At the end of my first year in the cadets, my commanding officer wanted to recommend me for a course that would help me advance to a senior leadership position in the cadets. Of course, I said no to that. It was not an option for me to attend leadership training and then take on a lot of responsibility. I made sure my father didn't find out about this opportunity, because he would have thought that I should accept it.

I loved playing cricket at school, and it was one of the things I was quite good at. But even though I was good at cricket and I loved to play, I felt as though I wasn't good enough to be on the team. By the time I was in Year 10 I decided I wouldn't play cricket anymore, and I applied to take up rowing instead. When I went to the first training session for rowing, the person in charge sent me away saying I belonged on the cricket team and needed to stay there.

After that I was forced to play cricket and my anxiety turned the game that I had previously enjoyed into a source of suffering for me. Basically, I felt like a fake and a phoney. At any moment, someone might discover that I should never have been selected for the team. That problem didn't go away when I went to teacher's college where I continued to play cricket. I remember someone saying I was good enough to be captain. All I could think of was various strategies to avoid that.

Another difficult part of high school was school dances. Our school had at least two dances each year, and there was simply no way I could go as I was far too shy to be seen. It wasn't that I wasn't attracted to girls. But the idea of going to a dance and asking a girl to dance, well, that was completely impossible for me. One time, a really nice girl, who was the sister of my older brother's girlfriend, asked if I would be her partner for her end-of-year school formal. She was really hurt when I said no, but I felt there was no way I could manage it. The idea of dressing up and going to her school event filled me with terror. It wasn't that I didn't like her; it was that I simply didn't have the confidence and my anxiety was too much.

Through the first three years of high school, I continued to have a strong sense there was something wrong between me and God, and I still thought there was something shamefully wrong with me. This led me to begin considering entering the Christian Brothers. I was interested in becoming a teacher, and attracted by the idea of becoming a religious person and serving God with my life. I had been taught by some decent Christian Brothers at school. It seemed as though having a life that combined both the religious and teaching dimensions would be the right path. After some soul searching, I was convinced that joining the Brothers would help me atone for whatever I'd done wrong.

Towards the end of Year 10, I told my family I wanted to join the Christian Brothers. This would involve moving to Sydney to complete Years 11 and 12 as the first step to becoming a Brother. My father didn't want me to do this. My family could see that I was struggling with school life and I needed to do something different. So, my father suggested I could spend two years living with relatives in New Zealand instead, where I could play rugby and finish school. He thought I could learn more about rugby in New Zealand, then come back to Australia and possibly play for the Wallabies! He was convinced I was good enough, but I just wasn't confident enough to even entertain his suggestion.

I realise now that my father was full of love for me and just wanted what was best for me. He must have felt that joining the Christian Brothers wouldn't help to solve my problems. But I was determined to join the Brothers, and he didn't mention New Zealand again.

I'm not sure whether anyone in my family realised the depth of my despair when I was in high school - my depression and the fact that I was not coping with my life. I truly thought that joining the Christian Brothers would help. Years later, in 2015, my sister and her husband visited us in Germany, and we talked about that time. She shared that she could see that I was desperate and that my personal anguish meant I was literally dying inside. We were a very poor family, and there was no way we had the money needed to go off to the Brothers, but my sister put the money together and made it happen.

It has been difficult for my siblings to engage with the journey I've taken to acknowledge my trauma and abuse. My family all live fairly stable, secure lives that are very different from the life I've shared with Leyla. I can accept that they are limited in their understanding of my experiences and their long-lasting repercussions.

Objective Witness: Constant anxiety

Why is it that Majnun constantly feels such anxiety? What is buried within him that he is unable to see? Why did he feel that he needed forgiveness, even as a child? Majnun's sense of shame stopped him from being truly alive. It was even behind his decision to join the Christian Brothers. He thought that joining the church would make things right between him and God.

Beginning to awaken – Majnun

I trace my awakening about the abuse I've experienced back to my diagnosis with prostate cancer. Since receiving that diagnosis I've been on a journey of discovery and healing.

Even at the beginning of our relationship, Leyla could see that I wasn't fully living – that I wasn't living my potential. She was right. Leyla often said there was more inside me that wanted to be lived. Most people who meet me see my friendliness and calm exterior, but Leyla could see right through that. She knew how vulnerable I was and how much I suffered inside.

I was first diagnosed with an enlarged prostate early in 2009 in Adelaide. The doctor who made the diagnosis told me to drink a lot of green tea and monitor my PSA levels! I moved to Frankfurt in October 2009, where my prostate symptoms escalated. My local doctor referred me to a urologist who diagnosed prostate cancer. The specialist proposed the standard intervention – immediate surgery. Neither Leyla nor I could accept that surgery was the right choice. I was only 60, and I was facing the risk of becoming incontinent and losing sexual function.

Leyla was the one who figured out the way forward. She researched alternative methods for dealing with prostate cancer. We met with numerous specialists, and we considered many different approaches She searched for information in medical libraries and researched men's support groups. Finally, we located a specialist in Germany who performed a minimally invasive surgical procedure. It was a process of finding a needle in a haystack and we both felt 100 per cent comfortable with that choice of the alternative treatment. Leyla was even accused of risking my life and had arguments with various doctors who wanted to remove the prostate immediately. It took every ounce of strength for us to go against the common consensus approach of the traditional medical profession knowing very well that we carried the responsibility in case the doctors were right. However, I trusted her research and went ahead with the treatment. It was exactly the right choice for me.

I believe the prostate cancer was directly connected to the way I'd rejected myself as a sexual man for so many years. The cancer was a physical reminder of all the things that were wrong with me. Definitely, a disturbing wakeup call!

Since that initial diagnosis, we have been on a long journey of discovery. I've had my eyes opened to the underlying reasons for my self-rejection. The safety of the container of our relationship helped me remember what had happened to me as a child. It bubbled up from deep within me, where it had been hidden for so many years.

Objective witness: Cancer as symptom

Was Majnun's prostate cancer a symptom of his self-hatred, deep shame and rejection of his masculinity? Was the prostate cancer a sign that he was ready to awaken to why he felt wrong inside?

Majnun had always been a 'good boy' – placid, accommodating, agreeable. His natural decision would have been to accept the prostate surgery as recommended by the specialist. But with Leyla's help, Majnun was able to question the efficacy of surgery. They worked together to find a better solution. He owes her a debt of gratitude.

These pains you feel are messengers. Listen to them. Rumi

Rude awakening – Leyla

My childhood was cut short when my parents separated. I was nine years old, and I wasn't aware that anything was wrong between them. One morning I woke up and my mother wasn't there anymore. My father didn't explain what happened. I assume they had a fight during the night and my mother decided to leave. It was incredibly traumatic for me and for my brother Guido, who was only seven. Guido used to cry for weeks for our mother, so I needed to grow up fast to care for him.

Our father was very stubborn, and he wouldn't let us visit our mother. He used to say that our mother didn't love us enough and didn't want to see us. My parents had owned a restaurant together, and my father kept it going, so he got custody of us. I remember our mother trying to see us once; our father said we were welcome to see her if we wanted, but if we did, we would never be welcome back in his house. We were children, so of course we couldn't go. We were caught between the two of them, and we decided to stay with our father.

I'm one of those people who can remember their birth, which is a bit weird. I tried Rebirthing at one point, and I saw my birth into this life. I saw the different furniture in the room. And I saw my parents singing and dancing. I checked it out later and my birth was just as I'd seen it. My mother was unconventional for those time because she took the risk of giving birth at home.

When I was very young, I had a speech impediment. Nowadays we would call it a language delay. Everyone thought I was mentally slow, and I was almost sent to a school for children with learning disabilities. I didn't speak until I turned six. I understand now that I communicated with my mother telepathically and therefore, I didn't need to speak. I mixed up letters and other people couldn't understand me. Even though I was a happy child, I felt alone on the planet. Other children would tease me because I couldn't make myself understood.

Just before I was due to start school, my mother took me to a homeopath for advice. That's something else about my mother that was out of the ordinary, choosing a homeopath instead of a mainstream doctor. The homeopath observed me for an hour and concluded that I was very curious and super intelligent. He could see exactly that I had not felt the need to put my feelings and experiences into words, and he suggested that my mother should sing every sentence with me. So, she started to get me to sing things after her, silly things like 'We will now clean the house'. Bit by bit, she levelled out the melody and turned the singing into normal intonation, and that's how I learned to speak.

That early experience has had a profound effect on my life trajectory. It made me want to learn foreign languages. I've studied several of them, always hoping that the next one would add to my capacity to express myself. I experience every language as being limited in articulating what is inside me. My love for foreign languages is based on the impact of my early childhood experience of feeling misunderstood and not really belonging to the human race. Even today, I wonder whether I'm capable of communicating my inner truth. However, many people have wondered how I have managed to master the pronunciation of foreign languages when I learnt them as an adult. Personally, I feel that is due to my inner flexibility and adaptability. Each foreign language allows me to express another aspect of my personality and I enjoy the playfulness of that chameleon state. Each foreign language allows you to voice certain aspects of your essential self and hide others. Since I have always been fascinated by what lies beyond phenomena, I ended up doing a PhD on the Silent Way of learning languages.

I remember being teased when I first started school. I still had trouble pronouncing certain words. The boys at school would pull my hair and tease me. When my mother found out that I was being bullied, she said that I mustn't be intimidated. She told me she didn't go through the pain of birth so that I could be teased at school! She always said that nobody had the right to scare me. On one particular occasion she insisted that I go out and bash up the boys who had made fun of me. I can see now how wise it was of her to not tell the boys off herself. She watched me from the window as I grabbed one boy after the other and hit them until they lay on the ground. They never teased me again. I am grateful that she taught me how to stand up for myself and fight injustice. She was instrumental in me learning Judo as a child. As I grew older, I moved from Judo to Karate, then Taekwondo and ended up practising Aikido as an adult. I hardly ever had to use my martial arts skills but having them gave me the confidence to venture out into the world. Confidence is an energy that protects, and I feel that especially as a woman I have often needed that trust in my capacity to defend myself.

A few years after my parents divorced, my father met someone else. My stepmother was the opposite of my mother and we had a difficult relationship. She had two boys from a previous marriage, and she soon had another son with my father.

So, at 13, I had four younger brothers and a stepmother who was overwhelmed. I did most of the caring for my baby brother Thorsten. I took him with me nearly everywhere I went, and we became very close. It's as if I did all my mothering when I was a teenager looking after my brothers. I made sure they did their homework and enjoyed spending my time with them. As siblings we would often make music together. I loved my four brothers and cared for them in all ways possible. I think because they loved me it was easy to get them to do what needed to be done. They sometimes ganged up against me because I checked their homework and made them learn French vocabulary, but it was always in good humour. My brother Guido once turned my bicycle, which I loved, into a tandem without me knowing it. I was furious. But he did it so he could go for rides with me. I realise now that my taking care of four younger brothers fulfilled any mothering instinct I may have had. That's probably why I've never had any desire to have children of my own.

Despite loving my four brothers, I was desperate to leave home as soon as I finished school. First, I moved to Paris for a few years and worked as an assistant teacher in a secondary school. Later I enrolled in the Sorbonne where I continued to study French and English literature. I also enrolled in more Russian courses. It might sound glamourous to live in Paris but for me it was a bootcamp in survival skills. As a young woman I was harassed quite often and felt intimidated by groups of young men who could tell I wasn't French. I was also unaware of the dangerous corners in this foreign city and being curious by nature I often found myself in situations a French woman would have known to avoid. For the initial three months I made sure I was home by sunset.

That meant I could spend my evening

reading and studying but I missed out on going to the cinema or theatre, which I had imagined. After months of isolation at night, I decided I had had enough of having my freedom restricted by men who treated me badly. I went to an army shop, bought spray cans of tear gas and got myself mentally ready to fight. I waited until it was dark, put on a trench coat, held one spray can in each hand and ventured out into the night. It looks to me now like the tomb raider in fashion garb. I was ready to defend myself against any man who approached me. Well, my energy must have sent a clear message. Nobody came near me. I walked alone in Paris until 3am when I felt my mission was completed. From then one, Paris became my city. Whenever I wanted to, I walked the streets of Paris at any time of the day or night. Always ready to fight, I had a feisty facial impression, never smiling to make sure any predator got the message from the start. Surprisingly or not, I never had any hassles once I adopted that mental attitude. I went back to that army shop a couple of times to see what else could be used to remain a free woman. The positive aspect of my boldness was that I met a number of American and British buskers and often we would meet in the Latin Quarter and make music together. I enjoyed singing and loved hanging out with other free spirits. The fun we had together helped me relax my facial muscles that I had to tighten up again to make the metro trip home in the early hours of the morning.

I spent one of my holidays in London, where I met a lovely Australian man. We got on really well and moved in together. I never returned to Paris but lived in Hammersmith with him for a while before he had to return to Australia as his visa ran out. On the spur of the moment, I decided to move to Melbourne with him. Once I was in Australia, I told my parents where I had ended up. I feel sorry now about the many surprising gasps I must have caused especially my father.

Accompanying my brother – Leyla

My brother Guido, who was two years younger than me, died in July 2007 after a long battle with testicular cancer. He had followed me to Australia and when he was 33, he was diagnosed with cancer. He was living with us in Adelaide when he died at the age of 44, and I spent many months caring for him.

When Guido was first diagnosed with cancer, I was living in Sydney working on my PhD. He phoned me from Tokyo, where he was teaching English, and told me about the diagnosis. He went into hospital for treatment, and his Japanese wife didn't return my calls or let me know what was happening. I didn't even know what hospital Guido was in. My PhD supervisor tried to help me contact Guido through the embassies, but we couldn't find out anything. So, I decided to just take a trip to Tokyo and see what I could find. I had no information where he might be in this huge city. One could say it was sheer madness to even travel to Japan but I trusted my guidance. When I arrived in Tokyo, I took the train that my inner self told me to take. The destinations weren't even written in English at that time. All I could see was Japanese words all over Tokyo Main Station. It was a foreign maze and after a long-haul flight, I was beyond clear thinking anyway. What happens in those moments is that I go into an altered state of consciousness. I tune inside and wait to almost be physically moved into a certain direction. A magnetic pull happens that pushes me to go forward. I took a seemingly random train overwhelmed by the foreign smells and sounds. About half an hour later, I felt the push to get off the train. I saw a bus approaching and ran towards it because I felt I had to catch that bus. I heard my inner voice that said to get off the bus after about seven minutes. I got off and then started running. I was beyond exhausted, but I ran and ran, all the time just following my inner voice. All of a sudden, I saw a hospital on the right-hand side. My inner guidance led me to the right floor and the right door, and inside I found my brother. It was incredible. He was as astounded as I was. But I will never forget his wife's expression when I appeared out of nowhere. I only said to her: "You will never stop me from finding my brother!"

After his first operation, Guido came to Sydney with me so he could recover. His wife stayed in Tokyo at first, then she moved to Sydney and they planned to get an apartment together. When she arrived in Sydney, Guido discovered she had been having an affair in Tokyo while he was recovering in Sydney. They hadn't been married long and I suggested he should leave her. But he decided to stay with her, and she forced him to cut contact with me. She resented our deep connection and the fact that she could not fool me. He went through chemotherapy and recovered, but went back to his old lifestyle. For a long time, she forced him to choose between her or me, and to my great sadness, I had no contact with him. I found that time very hard. I always felt very closely connected with Guido. Once Majnun and I were shopping in David Jones and all of a sudden, I grabbed him and ran through the shop to another section in the shop. There I saw Guido. When he saw me, he had a huge, happy smile on his face. I think his wife was angry to see how delighted he was. The spontaneous meeting showed me that we were still emotionally bonded and that nothing could interfere with our love for each other.

Guido 's cancer came back in 2005. He'd separated from his wife by then. He lived with us in Adelaide for a while, and we took him to some different doctors and helped him work out exactly what he wanted from life. He did a lot of walking and sailing, and followed a very strict diet, and the cancer went away. But then he moved back to Sydney, went back to working as a real estate agent, and returned to a lifestyle of stress and junk food. His cancer returned in less than six months. He found it very difficult to live a calm, healthy lifestyle.

He had a second operation and recovered for a while and returned to live in Germany. But two years later, the cancer was back. He decided to live again with us in Adelaide, first in hospital and then with us at home. I spent a lot of time with him and looked after him right to the end.

When Guido died, he was at home, at our house in Adelaide. I was lying with him, holding his hand, and I could see the angel of death – a huge black figure – waiting up by the ceiling. Guido took his last breath, and the angel disappeared. It was a sweet ending, but so sad.

I felt as though Guido didn't have enough positive force in his life and he wasn't able to stay healthy. Ultimately, I think his early childhood experiences caused such a deep-seated trauma that he became addicted to things – to unhealthy women, stress and junk food. Accepting that he's gone has been very difficult for me. I'm still convinced that if he'd stayed with us and followed a healthy lifestyle his cancer would not have returned. In hindsight I can also say that my brother's cancer was a preparation for dealing with Majnun's cancer. I had seen that Western medicine has limited options when it comes to cancer and was therefore much more prepared to looking for alternative approaches when Majnun became ill.

Objective witness: Human failings

Some people, like Guido, find it difficult to live a calm, peaceful, healthful life. We all have our human failings – the things that tempt us and the things we find difficult to resist. A spiritual path gives inner strength – a strength to live the lives we were meant to live, to work on the development of our souls, and to face difficult truths. Sometimes, the perspective of a non-human soul can shed light on the truth. Below you'll find a non-human tale – a story told by Leyla and Majnun's dog Elmas, using Leyla as a medium.

Look at animals as you look at humans. Rumi

Being a fur baby– Elmas, the labradoodle

This story is dedicated to Leyla and Majnun, my loving parents, whom I teach how to have fun. After all, they're only human.

'Are you getting up yet?'

I don't know how many times I have asked her this question already. Her, this is Leyla, my human mother. On her free days she likes to sleep in, and she does not realise how much that messes up my routine. I mean humans might like to do things differently on a Saturday and Sunday but, as far as I am concerned, and I think I can speak for all my fellow dog friends, I like my routines. I enjoy going for a walk at 6:00 am and I am sure to meet my friends at that time. She does not realise that when we finally get around to walking at 9:30, I will only meet strangers or one of my mates who had to suffer the same fate as I do: put up with late-rising weekend walkers.

When I finally get out, I see my friend Tucker. 'What, you are late, too? I tell you, I'm so upset with John, but he doesn't get it; he lets me wait and wait until I'm ready to bust. I wish I could open the door myself and go for a wander before he finally gets up!'

'I know, I know. I don't understand why they must live one way for five days a week and then turn it all upside down for two. Makes no sense to me.'

'All we can do is hope for the week to begin again soon. Monday is the best day for me because then I can have five days straight without change of routine.'

'Well, maybe we'll see each other again tonight. Maybe not. Given it is Saturday, most likely not. See you Monday morning then, mate.'

'See you and watch out for that big black monster with the blue collar – not a nice fellow!'

'Well, I'm not in the mood for scare tactics, so he'd better be careful!

See you Monday.'

Relief. At least one dog I know. His name is Tucker. He is a bit older so when I bump into him, he is the boss. His voice is thinning, not unlike his coat which in the old days would have been a shiny golden colour but now has threads of white running through it. His eyes still sparkle though, especially when he watches the white cat that usually sits on a wooden stump near the twisted apple tree. Tucker's owner is a middle-aged man who obviously grew up with dogs because, as Tucker has told me in private, he and Ben, his master, get on well. Tucker does not need to push and prod like I do. Ben picks up what Tucker wants without him having to waste too many words.

All the others seem either new to the area or to that time of the day. I keep on telling her to rise at the usual time, but I guess there is nothing I can do about her slothful habits.

I am Australian

By now you would've guessed that I am from Australia. Where else would a dog like my friend be called 'Tucker', which means 'food' in Australian? For those who like personal details, I was born in March 2006. All I remember of my early childhood is my time with my brothers and sisters in a glass cage in a pet shop. We played, ate, pooed, licked every two-legged creature that came to pat us. I cannot remember having any worry in the world. Well, I would have liked them to turn the lights off at times because I sleep better in the dark but, to be honest, I was not too fussed.

One day this kind man and his sister walked past, and it was love at first sight. I loved him and he loved me. I could see in his face that he would not normally gravitate to a white labradoodle, but my charm won him over. I liked him more than any other human being who might have been interested in my company and the deal was done. I was carried home in a dog mat, together with a fluffy soft blanket. It was sad having to leave behind my other brothers (all the sisters had left us already) but then again, it was exciting to head off for a new adventure, out of that bright enclosure and to sniff the suburban air.

Guido and his sister were kind and considerate people and I taught them straight away that I had to sit on their lap so I could watch the traffic. Thank God they understood that rule from the word 'go'. Once Leyla tried to put me on the back seat, but she got the message immediately: I was not a second-class citizen. My yelping and crying taught her to treat me with due respect. No, I didn't want to humiliate her. I only wanted to be allowed to sit on her lap.

My new home was a huge house with an even bigger backyard. Well, I could not turn the whole house into my personal playground at first as my legs were too short to climb up and down the stairs. I was carried, usually by this friendly fellow called Majnun. He also taught me early on that the sound of plastic bags meant that he was going to carry out the garbage. That always included an extra trip outside! Usually, we would end up on the lawn of the opposite neighbour and ran around in circles. Sometimes, their little chubby pincher would join in the fun.

Four people shared my space with me. Each one of them cared for me in their own way so I can't complain about lack of affection. Guido was my real master. However, as he was sick, he often could not play or walk with me as much as he wanted to. He taught me in the comfort of his room. He understood my language the best and I knew what he expected of me. When he put his hand in my mouth, he showed me how not to hurt him. That was an easy lesson to learn. We practised it many times. It was much harder for me to look at him. He used to say 'Humans look at each other when they speak. So, you must learn to look at me if you want to tell me something.' I used to look away when he talked to me. One, because my brothers and sisters would consider it rude if I stared at them; two, because I first had to get used to the weird habits of humans. Well, Guido showed me the ways of the two-legged creatures and my mastery was applauded by everyone in the house.

The women in the house were, as mentioned before, Leyla, Guido's sister, and Kader, Guido's girlfriend. Kader gave me my name, Elmas, which means white

diamond in Turkish. Leyla took me everywhere in the car and later, showed me how to not be scared of cats. She chased the tabby cat with me that always used to frighten me as soon as we walked around the corner of Cadna Street. Now I'm no longer worried by cats. Well, to be honest, I never catch them because I cannot climb as high as they can, but they cannot stop me in my tracks either.

Life with humans

But my master didn't get any better and he spent lots of time in the hospital. This meant that my daily rhythm became irregular and many times I waited in the hospital carpark for one of them to return and drive back home. The car became my kennel. Thank God I could sleep in it most of the time so that I could run around in the backyard once we got home.

Only one time was I allowed to get into the hospital. I was so happy to sit on Guido's bed and it was obvious how much he had missed me. We kissed each other so much. After a few hours, Leyla sneaked me out of the hospital again in a big shopping basket. When Guido came home, he only had a few more days to live. I could tell because he smelled in a particular way. He cuddled me but his energy was not the same anymore. The great spirit was pulling the force out of his suffering body. He still looked at me with intense love, promising me to look after me in a different way and then he was gone. I felt sick to the core. I vomited all over the place. I was so sad to lose him.

That was not a happy time in the house. Leyla was concentrating on her brother, Kader on her boyfriend, Majnun on his brother-in-law. I felt like an extra and only got attention when I was vomiting yet again. No good dwelling on the past but humans don't realize that we suffer just as much when a person we love dies as they do. We just don't cry.

After Guido's death, life was not much fun. Well, for a few months the house felt empty and sad. Leyla took me on as her favourite companion and Kader took me for walks. Majnun, as always, played with me when it was rubbish time.

My favourite place was the beach. I could run and run and chase balls and go bodysurfing. The salt water cleared my skin, made me thirsty and washed away my loss. The Australian blue skies, the warm sunrays, the happy kids on the beach throwing Frisbees – they all helped me getting oriented in the new circumstances.

The next person who left my life was Kader – she went somewhere far away, and I never saw her again. With her my long runs along the beach stopped. That left two humans in my world. What really knocked me for a six was when Leyla also left for long periods at a time. She talked about her 'father'; God knows who that one was. The minute I saw her getting that big suitcase out I knew that this was bad news. Mind you, she always came back but, in the meantime, life with Majnun was not exactly fun. He would drive off early in the morning, leave me in the yard and come back when the sun was going down. He sometimes took me with him, to a real fun place where lots of kids wanted to play with me. But that was not too often. Most of my days I spent lying in the backyard, chasing the odd rabbit, and waiting and waiting for someone to come home and play with me.

Well, you might think that my life in Australia got reduced to a boring existence as a suburban hound with nothing to look forward to. This would have been true if it hadn't been for the half-hourly trains that drove past behind the house and that I could chase until the corner of the fence. And, not to mention the little creepy crawlies I found under the rocks and the odd rabbit who thought he could make my yard his own. Life wasn't without its adventures. I just missed the humans I was used to.

My trip to Europe

Well, my beloved two and four-legged friends, nothing could have prepared me for the changes that were about to take place. One day, when I first saw Leyla not only dig out one suitcase but several, I got a funny feeling in my tummy. But then, when boxes were spread out in the middle of the downstairs lounge room that were filled over several days, I knew we were not dealing with the usual 'come and go' scenario. My stomach really turned when muscly men dressed in blue overalls arrived who one after another carried the boxes into the long noisy truck outside. Leyla mumbled something about moving to a new home but why should I care? I already had my home in Adelaide, why move somewhere else? My friends, I cannot tell you how much I panicked when Majnun brought home a crate, a huge one, red and white and asked me to hop inside. No way would I go into that thing!! Yuk, it smelled offensively of new plastic; it was cold and uninviting. He put a sausage inside it, hoping to bribe me. Who does he think I am? A stupid dog who falls for the treat trick? No way. Leyla was less considerate and just pushed me inside. Once I was in, I thought I might as well enjoy the sausage and then get out again.

That night they put my favourite blanket into the crate. Since it was pretty cold, I eventually got inside, making sure my head was outside the grille so they could not lock me inside! At least the smell was now more familiar.

This sausage-in-crate game continued for a few days and I slowly accepted the monster although, mind you, I never liked it. Honestly, who on earth would like to lie in a plastic box when a soft mattress with fluffy blanket in complete freedom is the alternative? Well, it became obvious that those two were preoccupied with something big. While I was a bit worried, I sensed that this time I would not be left behind so basically all was good.

I knew that something weird was going on when Leyla got up early one morning. That is never a positive sign and if it happens before the kookaburras start to sing, I have every reason to be concerned.

A yellow car picked us up, together with several suitcases and my now smelly crate and drove us to a huge open area I had never seen before. The big birds did not look familiar but neither threatening. I couldn't get any food down and to be truthful, I am not sure if I was given any that particular day. Leyla got herself a coffee but by the look on her face, I am pretty sure she did not feel much like eating either.

If you think the day had already been unpredictable enough, let me tell you that more surprises, unimaginable to me, were waiting. I got pushed into THAT crate again, now lined with newspaper (may I add that I am illiterate!) and before I knew what was happening to me, I was in a dark room together with a horse and three galas. The noise was unpleasant, a mix of mechanical and crazy birds' screeches. The black horse was mostly quiet, probably due to some sedation I would have killed for. I felt scared at times, excited at others, resigned to my fate most of the time. The dark room was loud until a friendly woman came, spoke to me, patted me, and gave me some water to drink. And then we got moving. 'Leyla, where are you? Why aren't you in here with me? What is this?' I kept on asking but neither an answer nor Leyla came.

To be fair, I think I slept most of the time which seemed endless. When the trip was finally over, all I wanted to do was to see my human masters again. I had missed them so much and I was not sure what to expect when the crate was lifted onto a conveyor belt. The air smelled different; the birds sounded more subdued. Where on earth was I? When Majnun and Leyla finally came to pick me up, they patted me and said: 'Welcome to Frankfurt, Elmas.'

When will you begin that long journey into yourself? Rumi

Germanic order– Leyla

After Guido died in July 2007, I wanted to get away from Adelaide. Every corner of our house, every street in Adelaide reminded me of Guido and the pain of losing him. I also started to worry a lot about my parents. I didn't want to be living in Adelaide if they were taken ill in Germany.

We followed our inquiry process (which we'll explain in detail soon) and made the very difficult decision for me to move to Germany while Majnun stayed in Adelaide. Majnun was still very involved in his work at the Islamic school, but I was at a loose end. Our online English-language business had closed because of trademark issues; I had stopped studying the Diamond Approach, and my work was mostly casual teaching jobs at universities. So, I took a job teaching English at a university in Frankfurt – a permanent job that offered some real security.

I'm so thankful we made that decision. I was able to establish a strong connection with my mother, and I spent a lot of time with her before she died in 2008. I was also able to reconnect with my father, and support him through his illness.

In 2008, Majnun spent an extended time in Germany on long service leave. Living apart was very hard and we started to ask whether it would be possible for Majnun to live permanently in Germany. He had trouble getting a residency visa, so that's when we decided to get legally married. The marriage certificate wasn't important to us; we didn't need a legal marriage to cement our relationship. But it was the logical thing for us to do from a visa perspective. We had a very simple ceremony at the registry office in Haan.

In 2009, Majnun was offered a job as principal at a small English-speaking primary school in Frankfurt. It looked like the perfect solution for us: both of us could work full-time in Germany, I could be close to my father and continue to work on the French PhD on Ibn Arabi I'd just started. But it didn't work out as we expected. The school had employed two senior staff at the same time, a principal and a deputy principal. Majnun was to be the principal, and he packed up our life in Adelaide ready for the move.

The school's new deputy principal started before Majnun. She was bilingual, and she believed she was better suited to the principal's job. When Majnun arrived for work, he discovered she had taken the principal's office and already established herself with the staff and parents. Majnun accepted the smaller office and started work, but was immediately undermined by the deputy.

With his lack of German, he couldn't communicate clearly with the parents. Within six weeks, Majnun was out of work and our big move to Germany was a failure.

Right through the winter of 2009–10, Majnun was unemployed in Frankfurt while I worked full-time teaching English at the University of Frankfurt. I also tried to make progress on my PhD. It was a very difficult time for us. Majnun became depressed, and we were under a lot of financial strain.

Eventually, Majnun found teaching work at an international school. It was an excellent job. The only downside was the distance: it was 80 kilometres from our home in Frankfurt. For months, he drove the 160-kilometre round trip to work every day. Eventually he secured a job at a big international school in Frankfurt and life settled into a much easier pattern for us.

Objective witness: Changing times

This was a time of great upheaval and change for both Leyla and Majnun. Leyla nursed her brother through the final days of his illness, then made the difficult decision to move to Germany – which gave her a secure job and closer ties with her parents, but took her away from her soulmate Majnun. Majnun achieved what he needed to do at the school in Adelaide and was ready to begin a new life in Germany, but his plans soon fell apart. Upheaval is bringing them closer to awakening. Below, Leyla reflects on her move to Frankfurt – without Majnun.

Adventures in Germany – Leyla

'So, how do you think you'll cope with living in Germany,' one of the American interviewers asked on this cold and grey winter day in Frankfurt.

'To be honest, I am not sure, but I'm ready to give it go,' I said, 'Australians are known for trying everything at least once.'

They smiled in recognition of their own situations. Making a country your new home implies a willingness to juggle the balls of belonging, homesickness, and cultural incomprehension for at least a certain time. Wherever you are, you are neither fully at home, nor a stranger. I could see that they had been through the mill themselves. I was in a similar position to the Canadian, the American and the German interviewers who had all lived overseas. I felt at home amongst this bunch of weirdos.

After that lengthy interview, enlivened by the very fact that it was over (who likes interviews, anyway) and the excellent impressions of the snow-covered university campus, I drove back to my friend's place near Cologne to get ready to depart for Australia the next day. Call me crazy. It seemed nuts to drive down to Frankfurt for the interview, back up to Cologne, back down to Frankfurt Airport – all within 24 hours. I didn't expect anything, to be honest; I thought of the interview as a practice run for the new job, I wanted to look for back home in Adelaide.

Back on the plane home the next day, I was happy to vege out, watch some movies, pop a sleeping pill (my chemical upgrade – one has to do something to cope with economy seats for 27 hours) and, of course, I did not waste one further thought on that interview. My husband was happy to see my sun-deprived face again at the other end, our dog did a few extra turns at the front door (I actually think he wet himself, he was so excited) and off it was to a few days of jetlag, which in my case means sandwiches in the middle of the night, high energy until about 2:00 pm and then zombie-like states in the early afternoon. I've flown across the globe so many times and all the good advice given by well-meaning mates, professional business travellers and flight attendants amount to nothing in my case. I get tired. Full stop. And when I am tired, I sleep. Period. I just know that about one week of my life is close to being wasted. My husband has learned to be patient when I wake him in the middle of the night to have a chat yet can't do the grocery shopping at 3:00 pm.

'Ah well', he usually muses, 'eventually, life will fall into place again and until then we'll just weather the storm.'

I was not even over the roughest parts of that jetlag upheaval when the news came that I had been selected for the job at Frankfurt University.

'What, you've got to be joking!' was my first reaction. 'Ah well, I'll just have to cancel them; nice to know that I got it. Good for the ego.' I was glad I could still do well in interviews, as it seemed like a good omen for my new job in Australia. Back to sleep.

What was that job for exactly? I began to wonder. Teaching English, yes, how, what, when? My mind tried to recall the details of the ad I had read a week ago. No recall possible. Back to the email. I re-read it again in the middle of my day, my husband's night. I noticed that it was permanent job.

Hey, do things like that still exist somewhere on this planet? I wondered. I couldn't remember having heard the word 'permanent' in combination with 'job' for yonks. It conjured up images of public servants, pencil pushers, lazy bastards, dead wood floating forever in some smelly government institution, cafeterias filled with middle-aged men and women waiting for the rosy days of retirement to come about. Yuk.

Not my cup of tea anyway, I thought to myself. I like flexibility. I'm a free spirit. I change jobs when they have outlived their use-by date. I move cities, even countries and continents to be free and have adventures. Permanency is not part of my vocabulary and please can someone promise to shoot me should I ever strive for it? So, back to bed, that job wasn't worth worrying about. Tomorrow I shall write them a lovely thank-you note. I did feel a fuzzy gratitude to those weirdos on the selection committee though.

I woke up my husband, dear old soul; he is the most patient man on earth, and he must put up with my shenanigans.

'Hey, did you know they offered me the job?' I asked him while he was still in la-la land.

'What job,' he asked. 'What are you talking about?'

'Well, remember that interview in Frankfurt, the one I squeezed in before getting on the plane. Come to think of it, I think it was about three days ago, well, may be a bit longer, but not much, anyway, it is a permanent job and they have chosen me.'

While I was talking, it occurred to me that I had probably been the only applicant. Yes, that must be it! Instant blow to the ego when I realised that there was nothing to be proud of. I did not see anyone hanging around outside that fateful office which, I must admit, had good views of the Frankfurt skyline. My husband mumbled something about me and permanency not going well together to which I had to agree. That was his two bobs' worth. And off he went again into the never-never. He's got the best nervous system on earth, I swear.

I, on the other hand, kept on thinking. It's one of my bad habits – to start thinking at night. I am too busy during the day – that is when I just function and flitter around from one task to the next. But at night, I think. Teaching English to some German students. 'Well, that is straightforward,' I thought. 'I have lots of experience and usually I get on well with people.' It would mean living in Europe for a bit again which I had wanted. Suddenly, I remembered that secret little wish that had arisen in me when I had to say good-bye to friends a few days beforehand. God must have taken notice of that wish. That is why this job offer came about. I do believe in wishes being granted if one only asks. Hmm, if this is the case, better not send a thank you note immediately, but contemplate the next step a bit more carefully.

The next day I did a bit of googling about Frankfurt. On the internet, all cities look amazing because no one takes the time to write a review about them. Buy a used book on Amazon or book a hotel anywhere in the world and you'll see subjective ratings that you can choose to trust or not. However, there is no option to give a city four stars, a triple A or a zero plus. Next, I researched the expat pages, but they tended to focus on giving advice about schooling, where to buy a car and which dentist to avoid. Obviously, the new arrivals have get-togethers, which as an experienced expat I promised myself I'd go to, knowing deep down that in the end, I never would. I mean, why would you choose to hang out with Australians that, back home, you would avoid like a pest? But the Dachcafe parties looked exciting and I promptly signed up for their newsletter. The next day I wished I hadn't!

What is there to say about Frankfurt or any city for that matter, other than that on official city sites it looks like a welcoming place, where people smile, and dogs wag their tails? Frankfurt seemed to offer plenty of lush parks. It was a far cry from the grey city I had landed in about a hundred times, whose astounding maze of autobahns always left me dumbfounded. On previous occasions, I had gone to Frankfurt in the middle of winter (our Australian summer and main holiday season) and had always felt 'oh so cold', so freezing cold, so unbearably cold there that I did not particularly like the place, simply because I need sunshine and beach. Well, that day on the internet I discovered the restored old parts of town, the Palm Garden, stately museums well worth a visit, a river that looked fresh and clean and many happy people enjoying the sunshine in the parks. My curiosity was kindled.

Maybe I should…?

Nonsense, I told myself. Frankfurt? Become a Frankfurter? Ha, maybe I should become a Hamburger instead. Ha-ha. Forget it. Life is good in Adelaide, the beach is clean, people are simple and cheerful, the coffee in the Italian cafes on Rundle Street better than in Rome. Why on earth should I move to Frankfurt?

I went back for another sleep in the middle of the day. Something kept nagging at me. The prospect of a new experience, curiosity, adventure, the thought of living again in Europe – it was all stirring in me and yet none of it was the final reason why I wrote an email asking for more details. In all earnestness I could not say why something in me pushed me to keep the door open.

When we ask for more details in Australia, we usually mean, 'what's the salary?' Not so in Germany. BAT 2A, it said. God knows what that comes out to. I tried to figure it out on the Internet. Those pages explaining a complicated, state-based salary structure were not that friendly anymore. They listed extra pay for living in certain cities but did not explain what it meant exactly for Frankfurt. Health insurance, tax deductions, everything was listed but no exact salary figures. It was all an enigma to me. I gave up. I could not figure out what it all meant and put it in the too hard basket. Why is this salary business so obscure? In Australia they tell you how much you will get in the hand every fortnight and that is that. Simple and straightforward. Well, it did not scare me because, let's face it, such a job you don't do for the money. If money is the objective, teaching is the wrong profession.

At about 1:00 am, I brought it up again with my husband.

'What do you think?' I asked him. 'We could live in Europe for a while. Frankfurt is central. Apparently, it only takes 3 hours and a bit and you're in Paris.'

'If that's what you want to do, then it's fine by me,' he replied and tried to go back to sleep. But I didn't let him.

'Yes, ok, but what do YOU think about it? Would you like to live in Germany?' I wanted a clear answer.

'Hmmm, I am not that keen on Germany, but it does have its geographical advantages.'

Men. Never ask them what they think. I could see the decision was mine and mine alone.

The next day I got this 'what the heck' feeling and my adventurous self won the internal battle. Maybe we just want to believe that we are in control of our lives and, in reality, certain experiences are meant to happen so we can learn our lessons. I felt a pull to give this Europe thing a go and although the thought of packing up again and heading back to grey Frankfurt within the next couple of weeks was scary, it was also exhilarating.

My husband took my decision in his stride. Elmas stopped wagging his tail when he saw that the suitcase came out of the walk-in-robe again. I was a bit shaky, yet more and more ready for an adventure. My friends took it on the chin. Good Aussies let you go, knowing that eventually you'll get it out of your system and be back. After all, we will always call Australia home. At least, so they say.

On the way to Adelaide Airport, it was over 40 degrees and the handle of my suitcase could only be pulled with a towel wrapped around it. I almost felt relief at the thought of winter. Mind you, I only had one coat that I never used in Australia and it proved to be a cheap imitation of the double-layer insulation gear needed to protect against pneumonia in Germany. Saying goodbye to my husband was one of the hardest things to do, as we did not know when we would see each other again.

My plane trip back over was not as happy as I had hoped. Heading into unknown territory seemed fine from the distance but the closer it got to becoming real, the less romantic it looked. What have I done? I must be mad. Why would I leave behind my home, my husband, my friends and my dog? I kept on thinking back to my last swim in our swimming pool, overlooking the ocean, the intense blue sky above me. And now I was on my way to this cold, grey, unknown city. I honestly must have had a mental block when I agreed to being thrown into the deep end of this potential morass.

The first culture shock happened at passport control when I looked at the officers not as strangers but representatives of a culture I'd have to cope with more frequently in the future.

Why are they so grumpy? I thought to myself. How about a bit of a smile?

In comparison to the guys at Adelaide Airport, these officers sent the signal that they meant business. Serious business. It was a first indicator that those happy people in the Frankfurt parks must have been paid models. Not many people seemed to smile without being paid for it in this city. I could only hope that their grumpy mood was only due to the extra-cold winter.

It wasn't. Germans in general take life very seriously. Life for them is not a laughing matter. It took me many months to realise that the Australian light-hearted attitude towards life could not be superimposed on this culture. Many encounters with civil servants whose stamps I needed in order to get settled in this strange country have convinced me that Germans love stacks of papers, heavy wooden desks, and collections of important stamps. They subscribe to the philosophy that work is meant to be serious, complex and above all organised according to rules written by stony faces on environmentally friendly paper. That dark grey paper sums it up and so do all these weird rules. Both I've come to hate. Not that life should be disorganised but, come on, let's be real, how many rules does a country need to function well?

When my husband decided to take his long-service leave and join me for six months in Germany, we had to contend with another set of rule-governed hurdles to get him covered by my health insurance and ensure he would not be deported as an illegal immigrant. Most importantly, we had to get his Aussie driver's licence converted to a German one. What I learnt in the process of helping him settle into the culture was that while there are endless rules, there are as many bureaucrats who have the power to ignore them depending on how they want to interpret the regulations.

'Sorry, we cannot accept your Australian driver's licence,' we were told by Frau Grumpy Pants in one office. 'You'll need to go to a driving school and take lessons!'

What? After 40 plus years of faultless driving, go back to driving instruction? He and I were thinking the same thoughts and fantasised about various ways in which to wipe this woman off the face of the earth.

'There must be another way,' I said to my husband once the initial shock had left its ripples in me.

We rang the authorities in Australia only to find out that you must apply for an international licence inside Australia but cannot do it from outside the country. Holy cow, this has got to be a joke.

Not being known for giving up easily, I suggested we consult a lawyer. How do you choose any professional, be it a lawyer, a dentist, or a hairdresser, in a foreign city when you don't know anybody to ask for recommendations? Well, my personal approach is to browse through hundreds of photos on the internet to see who has the kindest face. That's exactly how we found Mr Lawyer Wonderful. He wasn't just a kind soul, but one of the many Germans who also struggle with the arbitrariness of rules. He was smart enough to have made it his profession to turn his dislike of rules into cash.

There is a rule for everything in Germany and not many people who are willing to break them. At least not in public. My concession is that Germany is a densely populated country, and that rules and regulations help to organise the masses. However, even after five years living in Germany, I was still confounded to see one of those highly officious state employees pull out a book of rules and the highlighted sections show that he or she has actually read all of it! I can't imagine highlighted books of regulations in Australia.

The initial bureaucratic hurdles were challenging to say the least, but they did not dampen my spirit. I enjoyed teaching at the university, found an apartment that worked for a while and settled into my new routines.

Various cultural adaptation models show that after the initial honeymoon phase that feeds on looking at the new country through rose-coloured glasses, the new arrivals swing the opposite way. It's not dissimilar to the stages a romantic relationship goes through. First, the new lovers can see no wrong in the other one (one can blame a chemical imbalance in endorphins for this mental distortion), only to get upset about the ways in which a fork is held or the dishes are washed. For new immigrants, the length of each of these phases can vary but apparently, we all need to go through them to eventually settle into a realistic appreciation of the new country.

Well, I must admit that in my case the initial phase, fuelled by curiosity, lasted about three weeks, while the negative period, where I could only see everything that was wrong with Germany, went on for more than a year. In that time, I rang my personnel manager every second day to check how much notice I had to give before quitting and heading back to Australia. It usually went something like this:

'Hi Kevin, this is Leyla. I really, really want to go home as soon as I can. Could you tell me, please, how much notice I need to give before I can get the hell out of this place?'

'Two months, Leyla. You are tied to your contract until May.'

'Thanks, Kevin. Appreciate it.'

A couple of days later, I'd ring again.

'Kevin, this is Leyla again.'

'Yes, Leyla, what can I do for you?'

'Well, to be honest, I just wanted to check if it is still the same period of notice I need to respect or if there is any way I could leave Frankfurt any earlier?'

'No, Leyla, I am afraid the rules haven't changed in the last couple of days.'

'Oh, ok, well, thanks anyway, Kevin.'

Kevin was a saint, putting up with my desperate attempts of escaping Germany without ever losing his patience. God only knows what he would have told his mates about this crazy employee over a glass of beer. I give him credit for never letting me know his personal thoughts.

As time went on, the period of notice I had to adhere to became longer and longer. I eventually stopped ringing Kevin. I got used to the place and the weirdoes that have inhabited it for endless generations. It wasn't love at first sight, not even at second, but something has crept up on me that has convinced me to hang in here. For one, I love my work with the students at the Goethe University. They are engaged, appreciative, creative and extremely polite. Apart from that, there is no faster way to get to Paris than by the intercity express. Frankfurt is a great place for travel addicts. However, there are more than just mercenary reasons for making this country my home for a time. Let me try to explain.

While Germany is the top dog in Europe in terms of economic strength, it is the bottom dog on the likeability scale. Germans are not most other Europeans' favourite compatriots. Being an empathic person myself, I feel sorry for people who are disliked by so many despite their biggest efforts to show a whole continent their soft, compassionate side. Germany is sometimes not treated fairly. But it even goes deeper than a rudimentary form of compassion for this misunderstood culture. What I experience on an almost daily basis is a group of people who have high moral standards and live by ethical principles that I appreciate. Mind you, that does not mean that individuals don't try to pull the wool over your eyes. However, whenever I catch a student cheating, they invariably admit to the crime. They are compulsively honest. I appreciate the incomprehensible contradiction between seeing nothing wrong with cheating and yet admitting to it when caught. What does this say about their complex relationship to rules and regulations? My suspicion is that there is quite a subtle rebellious, even revolutionary undercurrent in their psyches that sometimes enjoys breaking the rules.

I appreciate that many Germans are loyal creatures. It might take you a decade to become a close friend but once you've passed the tests, you can rely on their loyalty. This might be because they lack self-confidence in being able to master life's challenges alone and have thus come to rely on outside supports. Their ongoing worries and fears tend to torture their minds. Poor little darlings, I often think to myself, why do they worry so much about events that you cannot control nor that are real right now? I almost think they enjoy an ongoing level of anxiety since they don't trust themselves if they were to let go. In my humble opinion, the German welfare system is the result of protecting against self-doubts, anxieties, and fears. This social security system is actually one of the most compassionate ones in the Western world, which is a positive side effect of their attempts to stem their basic fear of being left to fight the dangerous world by all alone.

My Australian background allows me to look at this lack of trust and diffuse anxiety with great incomprehension and yet compassion. Australia is full of dangers and hazards and you can get killed any time by poisonous spiders or other venomous creatures. The outback is not for the faint-hearted and even the cities are not safe at night. However, that is where the fun is. In the adventure, the unpredictability of life, the fragrance of danger in the air. And there is only one person to rely on in Australia, and that is yourself. Therefore, I can observe with sweet feelings of empathy the German attempt to control their environment by trying to gain reliable security. I can see the many conflicting sides of the German national character: their fear and their courage, their aggression and their submission to authorities, their cheating and their honesty, their cooperation and their stubbornness, their generosity towards strangers and migrants and their meanness towards the neighbour. Germans are full of contradictions and as I watch them struggle with their insecurities, I just want to take them by the hand and show them an inner landscape that is built on being at peace with the unpredictability of life. I want to give them a taste of 'she'll be right, mate'. I feel inclined to give them a hug to let them know that life is full of uncontrollable circumstances and that really, there is nothing to worry about.

Germany taught me to take my emotional, physical, and financial security more seriously. In exchange, I taught those I encountered to be courageous in an uncertain world. My sense is that this marriage might still have a chance of turning into a deep friendship and mutual appreciation. In fact, I know it will.

Objective witness: A soul's journey

Leyla's memory of her birth into this life gives us a hint that her time on earth is of profound importance. It is her opportunity to complete the work of her soul. Of course, the childhood trauma of her mother's departure presented her with challenges – challenges that made it difficult to settle her adventurous spirit, but also challenges that opened her soul to Majnun's reliability.

Every moment is made glorious by the light of love. Rumi

Sense of aliveness – Majnun

When Leyla and I got together as a couple, I was deeply happy. Suddenly the boundaries of my world expanded. I was introduced to a life where the unexpected and the unconventional became the norm.

After we'd been together for about twelve months, Leyla began to gently tease me about the narrowness of my life. My life was based in routine, and I put a lot of effort into keeping it that way, using all my energy to make sure my life was safe, predictable and controlled. I worked from home, seeing individual clients in my counselling practice; ate the same food for lunch nearly every day – Ryvita biscuits with vegemite, cheese and gherkin! I walked to the post office, bank, supermarket and doctor's surgery. Leyla and I walked together to the beautiful parks around Sydney harbour. But that was about the extent of my roaming. I was self-contained, living in my own little, hermetically sealed capsule.

Leyla was never like this. She was, and is, spontaneous and lively. She lives in the moment. For me it was confronting – both exciting and challenging. I had already taken some huge steps to change my life – I'd left the Christian Brothers, set myself up as a counsellor, taken an active role in organising Diamond Approach retreats, and partnered with Leyla. But I was still living a very narrow, protected life, with a predictable daily schedule. Leyla's gentle teasing made me realise it was time to be something more.

Meeting diamonds – Leyla

Majnun and I met through the Diamond Approach in Sydney in the mid-1990s. I'd been studying the Diamond Approach for some time, and I loved its teachings about a spiritual path.

I'd been part of a Diamond Approach study group in Europe in the early 1990s. When I moved back to Australia, I hoped to find a local group and I contacted the organisation in America to ask whether they'd start a group in Sydney. It was so exciting when I heard that a teacher would visit Sydney a few times a year to hold workshops.

I clearly remember Majnun arriving for an introductory evening on the Diamond Approach. He sat in the row in front of me, and I couldn't see his face. All I could see was that he looked conservative and sensible. But he was carrying an unusual bag and I couldn't take my eyes off it. It was a multi-coloured canvas bag, probably made in India, and it didn't seem to suit someone who was dressed as conservatively as Majnun.

I was mesmerised by that bag. It seemed to be a message for me, something I was meant to notice. However, I couldn't work out why I kept staring at this symbol of contradiction and was left with a huge question mark. Much later, Majnun and I decided the bag was our recognition sign. Our souls must have agreed to recognise each other through that bag the same way blind dates carry a rose. There's no other explanation for the way it affected me.

For a long time, we were just friends through the Diamond Approach. We often travelled from the workshops together, studied together and talked about what we'd learned. We gradually became good friends. There was a natural chemistry between us as though we've always known each other. Right from the beginning, we had a strong mutual understanding based in friendship. But it took us some years to realise we were soulmates. The crossover from friends into life partners happened naturally in late 1996. It was something that easily evolved. At some point, I just knew I didn't want to go home to where I was living.

We are very different people and, even early in our relationship, we could see our differences. I'm confident and outgoing, while Majnun is quiet and introverted. Back then, we didn't understand that his shyness came from deep trauma. I loved big cars and motorbikes, and I thrived on adventure. I'd been married once before, and I wasn't keen to be tied down. It wasn't until Majnun told me that he thought of me as a powerful black horse that shouldn't be fenced in that I felt confident he understood my need for freedom and travel.

One night after a Diamond Approach function when we were still just good friends, I agreed to drop Majnun at Redfern Station so he could catch the train home to Strathfield. While stopping at the station, some indigenous teenagers started to throw stones and bricks at my car. I wasn't about to put up with that! I've got training in martial arts and I'm not frightened of anyone. I ran toward the boys into the heart of Redfern, screaming for them to stop. They threatened to rape me, and I yelled that the first one to touch me would lose his teeth. With the screaming going on, some elders from the community appeared and pulled the boys into line. I told them off as well and said they should supervise their teenagers better. I turned around and couldn't believe that Majnun was hiding behind the car for safety! He wasn't about to run into conflict where there was a chance he might be hurt. It was an early lesson that I am the more confident one in our relationship. I can't stand injustice and I don't see why I should put up with being treated badly. Even when a situation is potentially dangerous, I will not accept being abused or intimidated.

I've never been able to walk away from circumstances that require a response. For instance, once I was riding my push-bike in South Yarra. In the middle of an intersection a man was lying on the ground and all I could see and hear was car drivers tooting their horns. Nobody had got out of their car to help the man. I jumped off my bike, stopped everyone from making unnecessary noises, told a couple of them what to do, organised an ambulance and then regulated the traffic until the ambulance arrived. I am just fully there in such situations and find it astounding that so many grown-up men and women can sit in their cars and do nothing but complain. Reacting spontaneously and taking charge happens simply because there is a person who needs help. Once the chaos has been turned into order, I simply get on with life. I guess that requires confident presence and a willingness to roll up my sleeves and get dirty hands.

Majnun isn't like that, and he's much more easily intimidated and remains on the sidelines. If something goes wrong, Majnun is less likely to feel the confidence to engage. He has become more confident over time, but spontaneous intervention is difficult for him because it activates his trauma.

Marriage or freedom? – Leyla

Majnun was interested in marriage quite early in our relationship, but I was unsure about making a formal commitment. I was determined to retain my freedom! In September 1997, I took Majnun to meet my Sufi teacher in Manisa, Turkey. I wanted to see my teacher's opinion of Majnun, and I needed to know that he approved of our relationship. Majnun understood that my teacher is like a father to me.

We stayed with my sheikh for a week, and he watched us carefully the whole time. He was busy building a house, and he continued with his work while he observed us. The longer we stayed, the more I became worried that he would say no. If he rejected the marriage, I would have accepted what he said and finished the relationship immediately.

Just before we were about to leave Manisa and return to Australia, he gave us his blessing. It was a last-minute thing, and we had a Sufi wedding immediately, with two witnesses. Majnun was accepted into our Sufi group at the same time, and my teacher became his teacher. That marriage wasn't legally recognised in the Western sense, but due to its spiritual significance it was much more important and real as far as we were concerned.

I wonder now whether our teacher could see we would have challenges in our future and that's why he was careful to observe us. Maybe he knew what was coming. Ever since, I've been so thankful he agreed to the marriage. Majnun is my best friend. We've been down a tough road together, but we've stuck to it. Even if we had known what was coming, I would have gone ahead without hesitation. Majnun is worth every bit of it.

Objective witness: Joining songlines

When Majnun and Leyla got together as a couple, it was like the reuniting of souls that belonged together and had been separated previously. They only realised this later, of course. They were meant to be together. In becoming a couple, they embarked on their true journey for this lifetime. Before beginning their difficult life's work, they needed to create a safe and secure foundation in their relationship.

Majnun has always been a deeply spiritual man, with a soul that needs spiritual nourishment. When nourishment was no longer available within the Catholic Church, he looked elsewhere. Leaving the Christian Brothers was an important step in his spiritual development. It was a brave move that took him away from the cloistered safety of the church. But it was an essential move if his spirit was to be set free. With Leyla's support, Majnun began to awaken to the full possibility of life. He was trapped in his simple routines, unsure how to move forward. But Leyla helped him to expand his horizons and accept a more varied life. It took some time, but he was becoming ready to embrace the journey ahead.

Majnun's soul was delighted to become Leyla's partner. It was what he had been yearning for, without ever realising it. But early in their relationship, Majnun held on to his predictable routines. He had already experienced a lot of anxiety and change, and he was nervous about taking on more. The first steps of his journey were hesitant and tentative. But challenge lay ahead, and he was building the strong foundation needed to face it.

When Leyla met Majnun, she was a free spirit, unwilling to be tied down, always seeking the next adventure. Majnun helped her to focus on finding the meaning in her life's journey. Becoming a couple created change for both of them, and they've joined in a place that you could call settled adventure. Leyla is more settled than she was, while Majnun has spread his wings.

With the Sufi wedding and the blessing of Leyla's teacher, Majnun and Leyla are ready to move forward. They have already begun their journey together, but real challenges lie ahead.

Being deeply loved by someone gives you strength, while loving someone deeply gives you courage. Lao Tzu

Freedom to be – Majnun

Even though we're soulmates and we belong together, both Leyla and I need our freedom. It's definitely more important for Leyla than it is for me.

Ever since we met, we've given each other the freedom to follow our own paths, take jobs that interest us, or travel when we need. I've always been careful that I don't stand in Leyla's way. Instead, I like to assist and encourage her to do what's right for her, and she does the same for me. She's been my rock and support and I don't think I'd be here without her. But she's also given me the strength to explore new opportunities.

Our choices in life have meant we've often been separated for extended periods, and that can be very difficult. Over the years we've been together, Leyla spent a couple of months each year in America studying the Diamond Approach. When she moved to Germany in May 2008, I first stayed in Adelaide. I finally joined her in September 2009. Leyla spent most of her student-free periods in the south of France working on her PhD. In August 2016 we moved to Perth where I could continue working. We have become experts at packing boxes and moving across continents!

Every day, we give each other freedom, support, security and absolute trust. The secure vessel of our relationship gives us the confidence to do what we feel we need to do., even when it involves being in different places. We cope with our periods of separation, even though we'd rather be together, because at times it's essential for our personal development to pursue an opportunity.

Negotiating Germany– Majnun

The decision to move to Germany was a huge moment for me. Leyla and I felt that we had lived apart for too long – with her in Frankfurt and me in Adelaide. We wanted to be together again, and I felt I had accomplished everything in Adelaide I wanted to achieve.

The move to Germany meant that I finally moved away from the things that made me feel safe and comfortable. Having applied for a job in an English-speaking primary school I was appointed as the principal. Moving to a foreign country was disorienting and difficult because I had to adjust to a new language, culture and climate. I left behind everything that gave me stability and security. Well, everything except for my relationship with Leyla, which is my most stable foundation.

I had only been in Germany a few weeks when I lost my job, mostly due to cultural issues and my poor German-language skills. Being without work for several months I found myself feeling increasingly depressed. It was particularly difficult because in Adelaide I had a job that was interesting and challenging and a sense of home where I felt comfortable. Somehow, I needed to accept that I was unemployed in Germany – in a foreign culture whose language I neither spoke nor understood.

One highlight of this time was the six weeks we spent living in Aix-en-Provence during Leyla's semester break. Leyla was working on her PhD thesis at the University of Aix-en-Provence, where she was given an office. Most mornings we walked to the fresh food market together, choosing what I would take home to prepare for our evening meal. She then rode her bicycle to the university and spent her days working there. I still remember the wonderful café crème and fresh strawberries before she rode off! Of course, I loved the aroma and colours of the spice stalls and the buzz and liveliness of the markets. Listening to Leyla interacting with French people was a source of great pleasure for me. She has an engaging, natural chemistry with the French.

It was while we were in Aix-en-Provence that I was invited to teach at the first German government international school, located outside of Darmstadt. It was founded by the German government to cater for expats working at the European Space Agency and the Lufthansa Airline Training Institute. It was an enormous relief to be offered work, particularly at a beautiful new school. Even though it was a long drive from our home in Frankfurt, it was worth the effort.

I spent three years working at the school near Darmstadt, mostly teaching the lower secondary students. Following that, I was offered a position at a European International School where I taught Geography, English, History and Ethics to senior years students. This job was a big step for me. Previously I had always avoided teaching Years 11 and 12 students, thinking the challenge was beyond me. The responsibility of making sure they would pass their European Baccalaureate weighed heavily on me and Leyla still tells me how traumatised she became because I kept on worrying about the Year 12s! However, not only did I enjoy teaching the senior students and related well to a wide range of international students, but I was also publicly acknowledged for my outstanding work with them.

Objective Witness: An expanding world

Our soulmates are now living together in Germany, embarking on their adventure, expanding Majnun's world. After a shaky start, Majnun establishes himself as a confident, successful teacher of senior school students. But challenge is ahead. We're getting close to his awakening.

As you start to walk on the way, the way appears. Rumi

Health turmoil – Leyla

The doctor who diagnosed Majnun's prostate cancer was a standard medical specialist who believed a radical prostatectomy was the only viable option. At that time, Majnun had begun a new job as a teacher at an English-speaking secondary school, and I was on semester break from university. I used my whole time to inquire into prostate cancer and researched the long-term consequences of all available treatment options.

I was like an archaeologist, digging, digging, digging for a precious finding. And the more I learned, the more concerned I became about the possible side-effects of the suggested surgery. I spoke to men who had experienced enormous difficulties following the radical removal of the prostate, including incontinence, impotence and psychological impacts. I also talked with men whose cancer had returned aggressively soon after surgery.

A radical prostatectomy didn't feel like the right option for Majnun, and we both felt alternative approaches might be better. But we couldn't settle on what was right for him. The research process was difficult, and we were under enormous pressure to make a quick decision. Because Majnun doesn't speak German, I went to all his medical appointments as his interpreter.

Every medical specialist we spoke to told us that this operation was the only answer. During one visit we presented another possible approach to our consulting urologist. He got very angry and insisted we must book the operation urgently. He suggested I would be responsible for Majnun's death if I didn't make sure he understood that there was no other option. But both Majnun and I had heard too many stories about unsuccessful surgery, and we didn't feel settled in our hearts. We could not accept that this prostatectomy was the only approach for us.

Eventually, I located the only specialist in Germany who practised an alternative method we felt was right. His approach was much less invasive – a sort of scraping out of the cancer without any of the follow-up treatments like radiotherapy. As soon as we visited this specialist in Stuttgart, we knew we had found our solution. We both felt settled and absolutely confident this was the right decision for us.

In November 2010, Majnun underwent the simple operation, which was so sought after at that time that men travelled from Arabic countries to have it done. The surgeon ran a private hospital and yet treated Majnun as a public patient. He received outstanding service, could watch the procedure on the computer screen as it was happening and benefitted from exceptional aftercare. While Majnun was being treated, I stayed in a convent nearby and could visit him every day. In the years since our decision has been confirmed many times over. Majnun suffered no side effects from the surgery and to this day, his PSA levels remain normal. He had all the follow-up tests done, and there was nothing. In fact, his PSA levels are perfect.

We don't understand why the mainstream medical system continues to insist on radical surgery with radiation and ongoing drugs. And we don't know why this specialist's methods remain alternative. Sometimes we wonder whether the money involved in cancer treatment makes it difficult for doctors to explore other options. Our process of inquiry led us to the specialist in Stuttgart and serves as encouragement for us to never give up the investigation until we know we have landed on the truth.

I believe that God loves the truth and used our hearts to keep digging. He led us through enormous inner conflict as we made a decision that could end in life or death. We were under huge pressure because every day we delayed the decision was a day when the cancer was spreading. But we trusted the process and continued to inquire until we settled on the right choice, which was linked to peacefulness in the heart.

Objective witness: The courage to question

Leyla's confidence that God would reveal the best way to treat Majnun's prostate cancer without risking his masculinity provided her with the strength needed to research treatment options and challenge the accepted medical wisdom. Leyla remained confident that the true path would be revealed if they researched and trusted the guidance.

We seek outside the wonders we carry inside us. Rumi

Guiding intuition – Majnun

Leyla has a finely tuned intuition, a powerful sixth sense, which she simply accepts as a gift. She receives internal guidance that helps us navigate the right path.

When we first met, Leyla was light-hearted about her intuition. Almost flippant, as if she didn't truly value or recognise how unusual it was. My first experience of her intuition was when we were in the Diamond Approach. She could penetrate to the essence of what was being said, really get to the complexity of it all, and then explain it to the rest of the group in a way that made it simple and understandable. Sometimes people in our group were confused by something the teacher had been saying, and it was normally Leyla who could offer clarity. Even when she hadn't been present in a previous session, she would walk into the room and already knew what had been discussed. Back then, I described it as a link to her unconscious, but I now think it's more profound than that. It's a guiding spirit, an inner voice, that helps her comprehend complex issues.

One of the first times I realised she has a powerful gift was when we met her brother and his wife while we were shopping in Sydney. It was a busy shopping day – the Boxing Day sales – and we were at David Jones in the city centre. The shop was crowded, and we were in the middle of looking at things we were thinking of buying. Suddenly, Leyla stopped and said we had to go immediately. All I knew in that moment was that I shouldn't argue. I needed to trust that she knew what she was doing. She led me right through David Jones, through the underground connection between the two parts of the store, and right to the opposite end. As we were going up the stairs, her brother Guido and his wife went passed us going in the opposite direction. It was incredible!

Leyla didn't understand what was happening until she saw Guido. All she knew was that an internal voice told her to go and led her through the store. Her inner voice guided us straight to the right spot, and the timing was exquisite. The look on her brother's face when he saw Leyla was incredible. He was so excited. It was an extraordinary moment. Inner guidance often happens to Leyla, and she just accepts that's how things are.

In the early years of our relationship, Leyla always kept two books on her bedside table – one on Ibn Arabi, the twelfth century Muslim poet, scholar, mystic and philosopher, and one about vibrational healing with crystals and plants. They're both wonderful books and they capture two of her great loves. She's deeply interested in Sufi mysticism and philosophy. And her interest in healing stretches back to her grandmother, who used to take her to the forest and teach her about medicinal plants.

When we were first in Adelaide in 2000, Leyla did a Pranic healing course. As part of the course, she had to practise on volunteers. The way that Leyla did it was very powerful, and it must have been clear to the volunteers that she had a special gift. They all wanted Leyla to work on them each time they came.

In more recent years, I think Leyla has come to accept her gift of intuition more fully. She doesn't take it for granted quite so much anymore, and she doesn't try to minimise it. But I still have a sense that she doesn't truly let it work to its capacity.

Objective witness: Trusting inner guidance

Majnun's experiences with Leyla's intuition and healing ability build a solid foundation to their relationship and gets them ready for the soul-searching journey ahead. Majnun is learning to trust Leyla as a guide force, not just as a partner.

Intuition – Leyla

All my life I've had a gift of insight, what you might call a psychic ability. I can see and understand things that are not always apparent to other people. It's not something I have any great control over, but I rely on it a bit and I know it's there if I need to use it. It just comes to me sometimes, if I listen to it without judgement, and it can be very helpful.

Sometimes I let myself see things, like the diseases people are getting, but mostly I don't look too deeply. Often, I don't want to see. Instead, I'd rather just lead a normal life. One benefit is that it means I'm difficult to fool, because I quickly know if someone is not genuine. Sometimes I think my insight comes with an extreme bullshit sensor.

When I was studying the Diamond Approach, their teachings helped me to make sense of my insight. They recognise that each person has certain chakras or centres that are more developed than others. It's not something you work for or earn, it's simply God's gift to you. For me, the centre that's most highly developed is brilliancy, which is an aspect of the third eye. People with this gift have their third eye opened and can see things behind the veil. It means that when there are complicated things going on, I can penetrate to the essence of it and explain it clearly.

We did some deep spiritual work in the Diamond Approach. I'd often get insights about the content, which came to me through visions. Some of the other members of the group were astounded by it, but it was simply a consequence of my Sufi practice. Our teacher in Sydney often gave complicated, multi-layered explanations of things, and some people in the group would become quite confused. Part of my capacity was that I could break it down and synthesise it into a way that made sense to people.

Sometimes my insight is very useful in a practical way. A good friend in Portugal had his laptop stolen and lost all his life's work. He had some tracking software on the laptop, so he could see the rough location where it had been taken, and he was desperate to get it back. Using my remote viewing skills, I was able to help him find it. By tuning in to the laptop and asking simple questions I was able to locate exactly where it was. I was able to identify which building, which level and even which apartment it was in. Additionally, I also knew that the person who had stolen it would try to run away through the back entrance. My friend went to the police with that information, and he was able to get his laptop back. The events unfolded exactly as I'd seen in my vision.

Another time my inner guidance was useful was when I tried to contact a friend who was living in Hong Kong. I'd gone on an adventure and travelled to Hong Kong by container ship, and I suddenly decided it would be nice to see my friend. The only problem was that I didn't have her phone number. However, I got some coins and started to dial random numbers from the call box. On my twenty-first call, my friend Catherine answered! She shared an apartment with a Chinese friend and would normally not answer the phone because she could not speak Chinese. However, when we met up later that day in Hong Kong, she told me that in that particular moment she had felt compelled to answer.

I can also use my inner GPS system to meet people. One time I had a friend visiting Frankfurt, and I offered to meet her at the airport. She wanted to give me her arrival time and flight number, but I knew I wouldn't need them. Instead, I just needed to be at the airport on the right day, and I would know how to find her. In fact, I just need to connect to my inner guidance and not resist when it tells me where to go.

Healing is something that I'm able to do, though I prefer not to do it too often. I have healing hands, and I make extensive use of crystals in healing. What happens in healing is that you open up the crown chakra channels. To do healing, you need to let energy from God run through your body. It passes through your hands, with divine support. But it's difficult to turn the healing channel off, and a lot of healers become burnt out from the energy that constantly moves through them. I've offered healing to a few friends, but it's not something I want to do a lot. I suffer with people because of the level of empathy involved, and it's not what I want to be doing with my life.

My most satisfying healing experience was with my father. He was very ill for many months, and spent a lot of time in intensive care. I was able to help him extend his life with my crystals, giving him time to do the work with his soul that he needed to do in this life. If I hadn't worked with him, he probably would have died earlier, and he wouldn't have ended up at the spiritual level he eventually reached.

I can't heal everyone, but often I can help people understand what they need to do to achieve healing. When I was living in Germany, a woman who was struggling with obsessive compulsions came to visit me. By looking into her eyes, I could see straight away that she was suffering from traumatic abuse. She didn't believe me – she said that it was impossible. But it wasn't many weeks later that she came back to visit me again, crying because her memories had started to return. I cleansed her energy and helped her to access her memories, but I could only take her so far. Therefore, I encouraged her to go to Istanbul for spiritual cleansing, because I didn't feel strong enough to deal with the negative entity that I could hear inside her. She followed through, went on the journey to Istanbul, and came back completely healed.

Inner guidance is a precious gift. And it really is a gift – it's something that's been given to me that I haven't had to do anything for. When I can use it to alleviate pain and suffering in people, I am happy.

Truth GPS– Leyla

I was brought up in a multifaith family. My mother was protestant, my father had Jewish background but was basically agnostic. Nominally I was a member of the Catholic Church, simply because they accepted any 'sheep'. Even as a young child, I can remember thinking the priest who taught us religion in school couldn't give me the answers I needed. Although he was a lovely man and was patient with my inquisitiveness, I often played up in religious studies because he expected us to accept his explanations, even when they made no sense.

Most of the teachings in preparation for communion seemed to be about sin and forgiveness. I remember the priest saying everyone is born a sinner and we must all constantly seek forgiveness. Having seen many newborn babies, I just didn't believe him. I asked a lot of questions, and he couldn't explain what he meant. It caused so many problems for me when I was young.

Before First Communion, I was expected to go into the confession box and confess my sins. I hated it in there: it was completely dark and horrible and scary. The priest asked me the same question again and again, about what sins I had committed and what I needed to be forgiven. I couldn't think of a sin I had committed, and I desperately wanted to get out of there, so I made something up. I told him I had slapped my brother when he'd done something wrong. It wasn't true; I had never slapped my brother. But I thought telling a fib might be justified to get me out of the horrible confession box.

Unfortunately, I was wrong! The priest wanted to hear more, almost as though slapping my brother wasn't a big enough sin. I eventually panicked and screamed that I needed to get out. My mother came running to me and the priest came out of his side of the confession box to see what was wrong. I was so upset, and I stood there telling the priest he had forced me to lie because he wouldn't stop asking me questions even when I said I had done nothing wrong. He was the guilty one, and I told him so.

After that I had my First Communion, and I was happy enough about it. I wore my little white dress and got communion presents. But the Catholic church didn't ever mean anything to me, and I didn't ever feel my questions were answered.

As a young adult, I became very interested in spiritual things and started to search for spiritual truth. It was a time when all sorts of ideas were popular, and I tried them all – psychodrama, gestalt, shamanic work, regressions, breath work, hypnosis, different forms of meditation and Zen Buddhism. I wrote out divine sayings from saints like Theresa of Avila, St Francis of Assisi, Rumi and Hafez, and stuck them all over my walls and doors, determined to find the true kernel of the human being.

For a long time, I considered myself to be a Buddhist. I didn't ever become a Buddhist nun or anything formal like that, but if someone asked me about what I believed, I said I was a Buddhist. While it sounds as though I was involved in many haphazard spiritual experiments, it's now clear that divine guidance moved me along the path I needed to take.

After I moved to Melbourne, I joined a Gurdjieff group for a while, where I learned about the conditioning of the ego and practised typical Gurdjieff movements to free myself from that conditioning. It helped me undo my automatic thinking and thoughtless behaviours. For instance, since I am right-handed, I practised brushing my teeth with the left hand. I wore a watch that went counter clockwise. If I observed any automatic behaviour patterns in myself, I tried to break them by doing things in the opposite way. Since the Gurdjieff movements require intricate and unexpected coordination of hands, arms and legs, I needed to be very present to not fall into automatisms.

I also practised Aikido, which is a spiritual approach to marital arts. As a child, I had studied Judo, and later learned both Karate and Taekwondo. I found Aikido to be a gentler form of self-defence. Later I realised how well it aligns with Sufism. In Aikido we use the energy of the opponent and manipulate it to bring that person to the ground without investing energy ourselves. We aim to achieve peace by overcoming the aggression of the attacker who is misguided when s/he is looking for a fight. Both Aikido and Sufism use turning movements and rather than being aggressive, the practitioner looks for the fastest road to mutual respect and peace.

I was always hunting for some spiritual meaning, for something that would help me fulfill my innate potential. It is clear that I had a great life in Melbourne, was young, independent and happy; taught at a language institute, spent a lot of time at St Kilda beach, had a big V8 Holden car and rode a powerful motorbike. Now I realise I was what you'd call a 'happy malcontent' – everything in my life was working well, but the deeper meaning of my life was missing.

In life, people often spend time stuck in some phase of personal development. As a young adult, I was stuck in the practising phase, being like a child with a sense of omnipotence who didn't understand limitations. I felt the world was my oyster, confident and had a sense I could do anything. Even today, I don't understand the sensation of fear that stops many people from doing the things they want.

Objective witness: Intuition and seeking truth

Leyla has an innate intuition, which she uses for guiding and helping others and discovering the truth in any given moment. Her capacity has been deepening, and she has learnt to trust it fully.

There is a voice that doesn't use words, listen. Rumi

Transitions – Leyla

I wrote this story soon after my father's death. It's about his final weeks on this earth.

'Look, Papa, you will either come out of this operation alive or you will die in the process. Well, in that case, you won't notice much and only we will know you are gone.' My father smiled at my directness and temporarily tried to forget that his chest would be cut open the next day to replace his heart valve. Ten years after having had it done for the first time. He took the news with great equanimity, shrugging off any fears he might have had in total surrender to the medical experts and their verdict.

'You are right,' he admitted with a grin, 'either I will come out alive or you will have to put on your big coat and say goodbye to me in the freezer.'

The following night was scary. In the early hours of the next morning, watching the time move along as the hour of his sedation approached, I was wide awake, sending him prayers and telepathic messages. We knew that after one year of having been misdiagnosed, having been treated with antibiotics continuously, his body had been weakened by this infection of his heart valve. I felt indignant fury at his doctor of over 30 years who had failed to send him to a specialist, had blamed old age for his ill-health and had neglected his fundamental duty to find out the reasons for his declining strength. Taking responsibility and learning from mistakes has lost its appeal in our culture that 'just wants to move on'. But, while the doctor could move on and possibly repeat the same negligence with the next patient, my father could not and had to pay the price for it.

Hanging around between the operating theatre and the canteen, both as white and sterile as each other, I kept on repeating my prayers for hours, calling on his guardian angel to guide the hands of the surgeons. In the early hours of the afternoon, I saw one grey-haired doctor buying himself a coffee and I asked him if my father had survived the procedure.

'There are rules in this hospital, and you have to respect them,' he grunted.

'But you are the one who can tell me if my father is alive or not!'

'There are rules,' and with that lesson he left me standing in utter amazement at such lack of compassion.

What has happened to humanity? Can he not see how his simple 'yes' or 'no' would settle my anxiety? I rang my husband in despair who sympathized and pondered if such a coldness of heart was part of the job selection criteria or the consequence of being a heart surgeon. Many worrying hours later I could sigh in relief when a chubby blond nurse brought the good news.

***

'Papa, can you hear me? It's me. You have made it. Squeeze my hand if you can hear me, please.' A faint movement of his hand made my heart jump. Yes, yes, yes! Thank God, there is some reaction!

'Papa, you have been in here for ten days now. You have a new heart valve. All is going to be good from now on. You will run marathons soon enough.' If only he could open his eyes. My God, I would give everything to see him open his eyes. See that knowing blue, that honest beam that he would project. Come on, Papa, please open your eyes.

'He has been through a lot,' the curly-haired doctor explained, 'give him time. I am sure he can hear you; he just isn't strong enough to respond.'

'So, you think he will wake up one day?'

'We will have to wait and see but I'm pretty confident. Go home now and get some sleep.' Sleep. Sleep. I could not wish for anything else but a decent sleep and yet it remained elusive. Fitful attempts at relaxing, interrupted only by my recurring wish he would open his eyes.

***

'Where am I? I'm hungry. Can I get some fruit, please?'

'Ha, you are funny, really. You have just woken up after two weeks in intensive care and now you want some fruit? Too cute. Dinner is in your tube. Steak and veggies tonight. All liquid. Can you taste it?'

How exhilarating to tease him. I could have hugged him if the tubes and machines had not been protecting him from human contact. He looked at me, winked his cheeky eye, two petty criminals who got away with it. Strong compatriots, in this together, silently in agreement to fight until the end.

I went home, ready to drop off into never-never land for the first time in weeks. He is going to be alright.

***

'Papa, what is going on? Where are you? Yesterday you were awake! Hello, hello, can you hear me?'

Something is wrong, terribly wrong. What had happened to the cheeky guy who wanted fruit? The doctor shrugged his shoulder, a slight avoidance in his eyes. What is he hiding? Why can't he look me in the eye?

'Why was he awake yesterday and now he is lying there like a vegetable?'

'I don't know, this sometimes happens.'

'What do you mean, it sometimes happens? Just like that? A person wakes up and then falls into a waking coma? Just like that? Or did anything else happen you are not telling me?'

The answer came through a Polish nurse who could empathise with my suffering. In passing she whispered into my ear: 'He overstretched him yesterday. He was outside the bed for too long.'

I cannot believe it. Another incompetent doctor? Should we be so unlucky? What happens to patients who are overextended after an operation?

For weeks, my father was carted from one examination to the next. He had tubes stuck in all possible places, X-rays, CT scans, MRIs performed on every part of his body. He was the object of discussions and pushed here and there by unfamiliar hands. Medications were tried to achieve elusive aims and others were given to counteract the side-effects of these medical experiments. He was a helpless victim of modern medical science and I suspect a welcome reason to charge his health care fund for a number of unnecessary tests.

I held his hand, talked to him, told him of the world outside, cheered him up, not knowing for certain if any of my words penetrated his subconscious mind. My feeling urged me to keep going between negotiations with the doctors and silent communication with him. My inner knowing reassured me that he was conscious, most likely of me, but probably of everything that was said and happening around him.

His helplessness, his speechlessness, his powerlessness drove me close to despair and yet I knew I had to be brave for him. This is not what either of us expected. We thought it would be a live or die situation, an in-limbo place of neither hope nor hopelessness. What am I to do? How can I help my father?

As the days moved into weeks and into months and one intensive care unit was replaced by another, my prayers became more urgent, my despair more wearing on my substance. Stuck between life and death, caught in permanent ups and downs, I became aware that my father needed spiritual help to either live or die. Something was not moving and if there is such a thing as free will, he was not making a decision. I trusted that he had his reasons for neither embracing life nor death fully.

Where does one find spiritual help for someone who had a Jewish background, had been baptized and then left the church, who neither believed in God nor in heaven or hell?

Shall I contact a priest? What is he going to say? Ask some Buddhists to chant for him? What about a Sufi imam who could read some passages from the Quran? Or a rabbi who knows the kabbala? Are there such things as secret healing prayers, formulas that one could write out in edible ink? Where on earth are the healers and spiritual guides when one needs them?

I prayed for guidance; I asked for help. I sensed that my father was stuck. Spiritually. Emotionally. And therefore physically.

Help came, as always, in unexpected ways. Weeks before in one of the hospitals whose stale smell was covered by a faint layer of disinfectants, I will never forget, a variety of alternative health practitioners had run stalls to educate the public. I had been attracted to the Reiki practitioners, having achieved the second degree myself in Australia about a decade before. I had had a little chat with two gentle, middle-aged ladies, then had taken their brochure in passing, thinking to myself that I could do with some energy cleansing myself. This unassuming leaflet dropped into my hands again when I was asking for assistance. Reiki, maybe that is the solution, I thought. I rang the number, explained I needed help for my father and to my surprise she remembered me.

'Are you the woman who visits her father every day in hospital?'

'Yes, yes, that is me. He is still in limbo and he needs spiritual guidance, I can feel that. Can you give him distance healing?'

'I am afraid I can't because I don't know if he'd want me to work on him.'

'Well, I understand but I'm pretty much attuned to him and I am telling you he needs help on another level. Western medicine is doing nothing for him anymore. If anything, all they do is pump him full of drugs. I've done hands-on energy transfer with him, of course, but am neither strong nor detached enough to be of much use.'

'Look, I'm really sorry, but you know the principles of Reiki. It is based on free will and I'm not sure if your father would want this treatment or not. But please leave your phone number and I'll see what I can do.'

'Thank you for your help and please let me know if you have any other ideas.'

So much for that one. What would they do if someone was deaf, blind and dumb? Free will – all nice and good but I am sure my father would like something to shift for him, but he cannot even lift his finger to give his approval to receive treatment. Well, at least she was kind and compassionate, so, let's see who else might manifest.

Five minutes later, the Reiki lady rang back.

'Listen; there is one person who can help you. Her name is Anne. I am going to give you her phone number. That is all I can do for you.'

'Thank you, thank you. I appreciate your kindness.'

Anne, I like the vibration of her name. Her surname sounds familiar. Where have I come across it before? Please God, let me connect with this healer and make it possible.

That night I went to bed feeling smithereens of hope. When I woke up from a quiet dream, I realized that one of my students at university had the same surname, Eton. I promised myself to check my class lists the next day.

Wow, what a coincidence. Or synchronicity. Such an unusual surname and yes, this student of mine must be related to the healer. Very interesting, indeed.

***

Wednesday afternoon. My language students cheered me up with their youthful chatter. After class, I approached Josephine Eton whose surname promised optimism among heavy clouds.

'Yes, Anne is my mother,' she said with a mixture of surprise and suspicion in her voice. 'Has she contacted you? Is there a problem?'

'No, not at all. She was recommended to me by a Reiki practitioner. I am looking for a healer for my father.'

'Well, I think you may have found the right person. In all my life I have never had to take any medicine. Whenever I had even the slightest stomach upset, she would concoct her herbal tinctures and oils, put her hands on me and it was all gone before I could even take a day off school. I have never been ill, nor do I know a doctor.'

Wow, good news at last. Let's hope the mother is a sweet and big-hearted as her daughter.

Anne emailed me the next day. Thank God, English was her native language, having grown up in Cameroon. I had learnt all my medical vocabulary in Australia. Several years of accompanying my brother through various cancer wards had turned me into a semi-expert in medical jargon. So far, I lacked those words in German.

Email: 19 January 2012

I got your message on my answering machine and tried to get a hold of you on Tuesday. My daughter told me about you yesterday. I will give you a call sometime this afternoon because I still need some personal information about your father. I will be glad to support his recovery and healing process. Please send me his birth date, full names and the address of the hospital and ward where he is lying at the moment. I will also need a picture of him when he was healthy.

Light and bright blessings

Anne

Oh my God, my prayers have been answered. Let's hope this woman can help him move out of his physical bardo.

I had no idea what her specialty was, where she had acquired her healing skills, or why she was willing to squeeze me into her overstretched schedule. Anne was a God-sent gift, and my gratitude opened my heart. Months of having carried these worries by myself had exhausted my energy to such an extent that any assistance promised a welcome relief. That night I dreamt that she was a traditional African shaman who was well-versed with a range of healing modalities. More relief.

When we finally met, Anne explained to me that she did spiritual readings for my father at set times during the day and the night. We started to work well together as a team. While she worked on the spiritual plane, travelling during her astral projections through higher dimensions, I kept her informed about news regarding his physical situation. I could also feel my own energy levels increase despite my physical tiredness and I suspected that she was sending me strength to keep going.

Email 23 January 2012

Bless you, Leyla. I am more in contact with your father, and I hope he will finally agree to come fully back with me on the earth plane. He is so hurt in our third dimension that he still needs more time, to understand that I can heal his heart. I told him I understand that where he is hanging right now is less painful, but I promised him I will take care of his pain, so this is what I have been doing and I hope everything will be alright very soon. I hope!

Hope. Hope dies last. What is hope? A sense that things will turn out well while being in a dire situation? An antidote to fear and despair? Holding onto a desired outcome even if the chances are slim. Hope. Fear. Despair. An ongoing triangular circle.

Anne asked me to come and see her, to bring back some of my father's hair and to pick up some vibrational oils she had made for him. I drove another 600 kilometres in a day to be the go-between and carefully delivered his hair to her in three different envelopes (in case I lost one of them). She also gave me her yoga mats and various blankets and cushions so I could sleep in his intensive care room on something warmer than the thin blanket I had used as a mattress on the floor. Knowing that I had some background in Reiki, crystal and pranic healing myself, she gave me a 'care pack' filled with a generator crystal, a pendulum for chakra cleansing, various precious stones and crystals to place on his heart and around his throat. I also got several bottles of herbal oils and wrote myself a list to remember which one had to be rubbed in where for which purpose.

Out of her absolute generosity of heart, she gave me a healing session which illustrated clearly to me how powerful she was a healer. I cried tears of exhaustion, felt the tension in my back dissipate and by the end of it, felt ready for the next stage in my father's journey.

'You are no longer alone in this,' she whispered in my ear. 'You may have lost your brother, but you have found your African sister.'

'Anne, it means so much to me to have you by my side. I don't know where this journey will end but to have company makes all the difference!'

With a huge plastic Peek & Cloppenburg bag full of goodies I drove back to the hospital where my father was lying. He had more stretches of time where he was looking around him and at me. My daily routine kept me busy. After a day of people walking in and out of his room, I felt the need to cleanse it thoroughly. I used essential oils of bergamot, rosemary and citrus to wipe all the surfaces, and then washed the walls and the floor. The fresh uplifting smell provided a welcome change for the nurses who enjoyed entering his room. After a few days, the healthy fragrances even permeated the corridors that usually carried the smell of old, stale, sick energy. Once the room was thoroughly energized, I started to rinse the crystals (one huge quartz crystal was under his bed) and took great care to prepare the pendulum that I needed to work on his chakras. I first did a general sweeping of his aura, and then moved from his feet up to the top of his head, cleansing and energizing one chakra at a time. The pendulum did all the work; it showed me where the congestions were, turned one way to remove energy deposits and then the other way to charge those chakras with fresh healing energy. Though I was getting extremely hot while working on him, I kept on praying. Please let this healing be to his benefit. May my father release all negative energy and allow himself to be recharged with fresh healing energy. I asked God, the healing angels, his personal guide and my guide for help and afterwards, once the pendulum had stopped moving, thanked them all for their invisible help.

Usually, this process took about two to three hours each night. I would then roll out my mat and tried to get some sleep, trying to ignore the face mask and the gloves I had to always wear. I thoroughly enjoyed those nights. He, or rather his oxygen machine that supported his breathing, filled the room with more or less regular breaths. Whenever he would breathe faster, and I would sense some anxiety in him, I would get up and either talk or sing to him. Sometimes I would just chant:

'One, two, three, four, all is good, you are not alone. One, two, three, four, your breathing slows down now. One, two, three, four, I am here, and we can sleep now.'

While chanting this at times for up to an hour, I would consciously slow down my own rhythm and sure enough, he would soon breathe in unison with me and go back to sleep.

My other task at night was to ensure that the permanently busy nurses came to him as soon as the alarms on his machines went off. Not only was it vital for him to get his circulation medication as soon as it ran out because once it had dropped, he would have to be topped off with an extra high dose of medication. These drips were a mixed bag. While they stopped his blood pressure from collapsing, they also caused black toes and fingers that would eventually fall off. I saw a number of other patients who had lost their fingers and held up stumps instead. So, I was very keen to make sure he needed as little of this poison as possible. I also wanted him to get as much rest as possible. Virtually impossible in the ICU or any hospital room for that matter. That is why I jumped out of my slumber the minute an alarm went off so he could be looked after and get more rest.

Anne and I stayed in constant contact. Either by email, SMS or phone calls. One day she wrote:

'I have fallen in love with his soul. Please let me know if the oils are almost empty. Then you could come and pick up some new ones. Please take care of yourself and make sure you take a rest when you need one. I am now taking care of your Dad, so you don't need to worry, okay? I am sending you much love and Energy!

God Bless You.

In Love and Light, Anne'

I responded:

'Dear Anne
I have just come back from visiting my father. His circulation is
still as good as yesterday and his breathing seems to be more relaxed.
I personally think his skin colour and aura have a pinkish glow. Overall,
the room is filled with green light. And some pink. Well, that is at least
my sense. I pray that he will be able to take the corner with your help.
He looked at me in a very focussed way today and I told him that he
will be well again. I pray to God that I will never feel like a liar! Love,
Leyla'

I do not know what my father felt or thought when he saw me sleep on
the floor of his room, move the pendulum along his body, talk to him
about his recovery, sang to him all the songs he used to sing to me, run
to the nurses to get help, chant him back into relaxation. He must have
felt amusement at times, but he would have also felt my overwhelming
love for him, my ardent desire for him to come back into physical life.

Papa, I want you to get well again. I really understand if you do not
want to inhabit this sick body anymore. I also accept if you prefer to
hang around in other dimensions than this painful earthly one. But, to be
honest, if it was up to me, I would like you to wake up fully, pull out
those tubes and say to me: 'Come on, let's leave this place.'

As time went on, I was not sure anymore if I had thought or spoken out
loud these words. He picked them up, regardless. We were
telepathically so connected that it did not matter if words remained
silent in our minds or were expressed.

While I was working at the coalface in the physical realm, Anne
connected with my father in the spiritual sphere. She passed on valuable
information to me about what he was telling her on her astral discovery
tours.

'You know, Leyla, your father has been hurt a lot emotionally. He
literally has a broken heart. Your mother was the person who cut his
heart in half and since then he has suppressed this heartache. This is
why he has had two heart operations and is now undecided whether he

wants to live or to die,' Anne wrote to me. She is right, I thought, he has always put on a bright face, cheering up all those around him. The sad clown.

'I am working on his emotional heart,' Anne explained. 'I am telling him that he can trust me, that he will never have to feel such emotional pain again. I hope he will listen to me and live a second life in the same body.'

I realised that I owed my big-heartedness to both my parents. I was a planned child; I was born at home and just before my birth my parents sang and danced together in the living room. They were so happy that I was coming out to join them. The trouble that happened afterwards and that ended in my mother leaving overnight when I was 9 years old was due to a lot of life circumstances and it damaged my father's heart. And my mother's too. I did not see my mother for 29 years! So, pain on all sides but right now, all that mattered was to allow my father to arrive at a new form of healing.

Can a broken heart be mended? Can a human being who has suppressed emotional pain for decades, who has caused physical heartache for himself and undergone two life-threatening operations to have the hurt fixed by surgeons, transform in such a way that healing can happen?

Anne drove up to see my father in person. She brought her shamanic bells, her potions and most importantly, all of herself. She said:

'Don't ask me why but I think he deserves a chance to experience love and happiness again before moving on to a sudden rebirth. I really wish from the bottom of my heart that he will give me the chance to heal him.'

My father must have been surprised and relieved to see in physical reality the African woman who had been appearing to him in his deeper levels of consciousness. What exactly she did with him while I guarded the door, I will never know. I heard ancient, archetypal songs, bells and lots of silence. And I saw her stumbling out all pale and ill-looking. I felt so sorry for her. She had taken into herself some of my father's condition and for the first time I physically saw in her what he must have been experiencing all this time.

'I have to vomit,' she muttered while rushing past me.

Oh my God, Anne, I am so sorry. Is this what a healer must go through? You poor thing. Why would anyone choose such a profession and such a life of service?

I did not follow her to give her some privacy. I had a quick peek into my father's room and saw that he had the most peaceful expression on his face. His skin was glowing. A pinkish tone shimmered through his naturally dark skin.

'Papa, I haven't seen you shine like this in months. Let's hope your African girlfriend can make you say 'yes' to life again.'

Anne came back up to the ward again about 20 minutes later, having lost some of her paleness but still looking very exhausted.

'It is his medication,' she said, 'he is full of toxins from this medicine. It is killing his organs. And it is making me very sick as well because I go into his body to bring about healing and I can tell you; it is no fun being in there.'

'I do not understand because the doctor had promised to stop all this unnecessary neurological medication.'

'Well,' Anne said. 'My body does not lie to me. I think it might be the doctor who is lying to you. And your father also told me that he has pains in his stomach from that medication.'

But this is impossible. The cardiologist in charge had promised to me two weeks ago he would phase out that horrible Keppra stuff that had been given in case he had an epileptic fit. Could it be that he had been lying to me?

'What medication is my father on?' I asked Andrea, one of the more competent and caring nurses that I trusted completely.

'Well, let's have a look at the medical charts,' she said, and we went to the front office.

'Doctor S. has stopped the Keppra but has replaced it with another one, Valporan, which he is getting three times a day, 600 mg each. I personally think he does not need it because he is very calm and quiet.'

This medico wants to kill my father, I thought.
I wrote a letter to the doctors who would be looking after him the following day. Andrea made sure it was immediately visible in his files. In it I asked them to stop all unnecessary medication and that I was disappointed that one medication was stopped only to be replaced by a stronger one.

I have had enough of the medical profession. My poor father! He is full of poison and then they complain that he does not wake up!

Andrea did not give him the medication the next afternoon but ticked it off as given in the records. Courageous girl! He then woke up more, his blood pressure was right again, and the circulation medication could be reduced. Three proofs that this neurological toxin was bad for him. I also found out that he was getting tablets for his stomach as Valporan destroys the stomach lining. Anne was right. He had told her about his stomach pains.

Anne, you are an angel! Papa, I will make sure all unnecessary medication is stopped immediately! I promise.

The sly doctor got into trouble for abusing my trust. He had to stop the neurological medicine and came to me to talk about 'some misunderstandings. There was no misunderstanding, just very different ideas about medicine and healing. While he thought, 'the more, the better,' I thought, 'as much as necessary, as little as possible.' From then on, he would have to ask for my permission if the treatment plan was changed.

My father regained consciousness and had many hours where he could look around and be present. Anne continued with her readings and worked on his emotions during her astral travels. I kept going with my daily routine of cleansing his chakras and his room. I spent every spare minute in his presence. Day and night. The doctor in charge avoided me and the nurses thanked me for having challenged him.

May this detoxification help him to get better. May the medical profession keep him alone so the healer can work without their interference. May those who are slaves to the pharmaceutical companies take their own poisons one day.

***

'Papa, how are you feeling today? It is getting warmer outside. Soon you will have your 80th birthday. You always wanted to get to 80, didn't you?'

He looked at me, trying to formulate some words but due to the endotracheal tube, which surely bothered him, he could only move his lips.

I wish I could hear you. How I wish I could hear your calm voice once more!

'Papa, you cannot speak yet, you have a tube in your throat but one day that will come out again and all will be well.'

I wasn't sure anymore of my own beliefs.

Email: 5 February 2012

Dear Leyla, your father is still standing at the labyrinth in the 4th chamber of the 7th dimension, where he has been the last three days. I am going to stay with him there for now, I cannot yet convince him to come back down. Love and light, Anne.

Papa, why don't you listen to Anne and come back down again into your physical body. What needs to happen for you to move? Give me a sign, please.

Anne was getting more and more exhausted. She told me that she was getting nauseous while working on my father. Although the medications were kept at a low level, his body was so full of accumulated toxins that she often lost her focus and concentration when she entered his body. But she wrote in an SMS that she was a health war surgeon and wouldn't give up in the middle of a health war.

I was waiting for telepathic news from my father. While Anne kept me informed that she was working on his emotional fears and feelings of jealousy, I kept on cleansing his body and sang to him for hours. My singing became soothing for both of us. Music, coming straight from my heart, beamed directly into his. I am sure he felt the immensity of my love for him and I noticed that we both grew increasingly peaceful. Life could have continued in that intensive care unit for ever. I was perfectly happy in my patience and he seemed more and more settled.

On the 8th of February, Anne noticed that my father had 'a guide with him. Angel Shihkina, who was helping with the healing.'

Peace settled more palpably in the room. My father was there, so intensely there that I felt at times he was seeing everything with X-Ray vision. The doctors who came in to check if he was conscious always caught him when he was sleeping or resting. I was not sure if he didn't close his eyes every time; he sensed them coming into his room. That would have been true to character.

***

'Anne, why did he make so many compromises in his life? Why didn't he put up more of a fight? Why did he allow his heart to be hurt in such a deep way and yet never did anything about it,' I asked her in one of our after-midnight phone calls.

'Leyla, only your father can answer that question, but I think he did it for a good reason.'

That night I saw it—saw his life, saw his inner conflict. Things he had done---things I had sometimes interpreted as weakness of character, he had done for us. My brother and me. He did not want his children to suffer any more than we already had after my mother had left. So, he sacrificed himself. He became quiet and avoided trouble at any cost. Yes, Anne was right; he had done it for a very good reason—us.

I had a quick coffee and then ran into his room. I looked at him, feeling deep love and appreciation, very sorry that all my life I had judged his sacrifice as weakness.

'Papa, I've got it. I'm so sorry. I've got the message. You did it for us. I can see that you wanted to spare us more heartache. I'm so sorry that I didn't realize that any earlier. Please forgive me. I'm so stupid sometimes. And thank you. Thank you for waiting for me to see this. You waited until I would get it. Thank you.'

He understood that I had got it. He was very peaceful.

At midnight I woke up from my increasingly deep sleeps. The night nurse told me that my father had been awake for hours while I was sleeping. He had done the fatherly thing—watching over me while I was there to watch over him. The nurse said it was very sweet and that I'd slept like a log.
Papa, you are through and through a father until the end. My mother had been right when she said that she felt he was the better mother. Oh my God, why is life so twisted and weird at times?

I sang 'Happy Birthday' to him. The room was filled with love, song, lemony fragrance and light. Light upon light.

'You have made it, Papa. You're 80! Yes, well done! I'm so proud of you. And you know, I want to tell you in all honesty that I'll never be ready to let you go. Never, ever. I'll always want to keep you here with me. Always. Because, what will life be like without you? You're the one who understands me; you know why I'm the way I am. So, why would I let you go? But you know what? I'll let you go. For your sake. Because I love you. You have waited for months so I could understand your life. Again, I'm sorry. I hope you can forgive me for all the times I've hurt you. It must have been so hard for you when I didn't ring for weeks on end or was too busy leading my own life. Please forgive me. If you want to leave, I'll let you go. It would be too selfish to not let you go. So, go if you want to. I'll accompany you for as long as I can and then I'll stay behind. One day, we'll see each other again. And when you get to your next stage, please greet my brother and my mother. Tell them I miss them terribly. They'll be so happy to see you again. You're the best father on earth. The absolutely best. You are my hero and will always live in my heart.'

The words tumbled out of me. He heard me. I knew then that this was what he had been waiting for. For me to understand his life and to be ready to let him go. He had waited, patiently, lovingly with kindness and compassion. It was my task to return the favour.

***

The day after his birthday the internal bleeding started to fill bag after bag. He was peaceful. Anne told me that he was already moving out of his body. He had looked back at me one more time but because he felt that I would be strong enough to cope, he had moved on. Into the tunnel, towards the light he felt pulled towards. I sang, softly, quietly, his favourite tunes. I told him that I loved him, that he was the very best father ever, I said 'see you later', and I encouraged him to go towards the light. He looked at me the whole time. He wanted to make sure I was feeling strong enough for his departure.

'Papa, I love you. Follow the light. You are the best. The best ever. I am singing you into death the way you sang me into life.'

He took his last breath. And our song continues.

Objective Witness: Channelling the gift of insight

Leyla clearly has a gift of insight combined with an ability to heal. She simply accepts it as part of who she is. Her father and her brother Guido benefited from her gift. But widespread healing is not why she was born into this life. As we will discover, Majnun was not just the focus of her healing attention in terms of the cancer but also the traumatic experiences he had as a child.

Out of suffering have emerged the strongest souls. Kahlil Gibran

Difficult memories – Majnun

For most of my adult life, I had no memory of being sexually abused as a child. I knew there was something deeply wrong with me, but I had no idea what it was.

One night, while we were living in Germany and I was recovering from the prostate cancer procedure, Leyla told me about a radio program she'd been listening to in the car. It was a documentary about the terrible sexual abuse that happened in the boarding schools of the Catholic Church in Germany. The program described the effect of sexual abuse on victims, and the enduring impact it's had on their lives.

Leyla was shocked by the personal testimonies of the victims and during her drive home she entered an altered state of consciousness because the long-term impacts described pretty accurately the way I lead my life. The minute she entered the house, she started to talk about the program and recount everything she'd heard. Almost immediately, I had incredible sensations of tingling and uncomfortable heat in my body. It was the beginning of my disorientation with disturbing memories resurfacing.

It probably took five years for the experiences to come to consciousness. First, I sought help from my GP who referred me to an English-speaking therapist. However, their waiting period was over two years and when I could finally work with a therapist, the language difficulties meant it wasn't very successful. I also did some ritual work with the shaman who had successfully worked with Leyla's father. Her approach was very beneficial because it included writing letters to significant people in my life. I had to recall as much as I could and then burn the letters in a set ritual. In terms of everyday functioning the help I received from a trauma specialist was very beneficial. I can say now that being able to express myself in English and working with someone who was familiar with the sexual abuse that went on in the Catholic Church in Australia assisted me a lot. I didn't have to think about the words I used to express my feelings and could rely on cultural connotations being mutually understood.

This was a very challenging period in my life. Leyla said that every night during that period I would toss, turn and twitch in my sleep, and my sleep patterns became very disturbed. During the day, I would get flashes of pictures, would all of a sudden get an uncomfortable body sensation and had unexpected feelings of fright and even terror. Nothing came as a well-constructed story. There were fragments, snippets and bodily discomforts that appeared and disappeared out of the blue. I lived in a state of fear because I could not control when memories would emerge and how they would affect me. Not being in control of what was happening to me left me feeling at the mercy of this unknown force that pushed the horrible recollections from my unconscious to my conscious self. It was terrifying at times and deeply disorienting for many years.

When I look back now, I wonder whether I was never meant to wake up to what had happened. The fact that I had to deal with cancer, lived in a foreign country whose language I didn't speak, work in an unfamiliar environment whose rules I did not understand -all of these new, disorienting experiences might have opened up the pandora's box. Maybe, if I had stayed in my small, well-trodden environment I would have kept all these memories under wraps. I guess that this is exactly why we travel and explore unfamiliar situations. We want to get in touch with aspects of ourselves that we have not made conscious contact with so far. Well, by going to Germany I was thrown in the deep end and my usual mechanisms of keeping myself and my world small didn't work anymore. Thus, the other suppressed aspects could emerge. I also think that the key has been Leyla. If I hadn't been with Leyla, there is no way that I could have ever felt safe enough to wake up. She provided the emotional stability I needed to face the destabilising memories and frightening disorientation involved in reassessing my life's journey.

Objective witness: Leyla as main support

People like Majnun have a lot hidden inside. Sometimes other people can see it, but most people can't assist in revealing it. Leyla was Majnun's support, giving him the strength to learn about what had happened. Leyla walked beside him and believed in him. She had a deep trust in him, which allowed him to discover the truth of his early childhood experiences and work through them together. Majnun lacked the capacity to do this alone, because he had been so deeply hurt.

Childhood abuse – Majnun

I grew up in Brisbane, in a poor, Catholic family. My father was unable to work because he had caught tuberculosis during the war. He was obviously very intelligent but also angry that his life had not turned out the way he had imagined it. I was the second youngest of five children. We all attended Catholic schools, and my parents were very keen to see that we were well educated.

When I was in Year 2 at the local convent school, my father spent a long stretch in a veterans' hospital and my twelve-year-old sister, who had polio was quarantined in a specialised hospital. My mother was trying to cope with two young children and two older teenagers at home, one child and a husband in hospitals in different parts of Brisbane. My older brother was attending a Christian Brothers high school and was an altar boy while my oldest sister was in her final of studies to become a teacher.

A parish priest spent a lot of time with our family, visiting us and helping us. He was a funny Irish man, and everyone in the family thought he was wonderful. My mother was obviously overstretched most of the time trying to keep the family together, looking after four children and an incapacitated husband. While mum visited my sister and father in hospital, this priest would look after my younger brother and me.

Often, the priest would take me and my little brother to a local park to play. It was a huge park, with a creek running along one side. Most of the time we played wrestling games, and while we were wrestling the priest would touch me by putting his hand on my genitals. It didn't feel right, but I didn't ever say anything about it. No one else would have been able to see what was happening.

We weren't allowed to swim in the creek, but sometimes if we had an adult with us, we would jump in and have a quick swim. I remember we went swimming a few times when the priest was with us, and he always helped me to get dry. As he was drying me, he would play with my penis. He was very subtle about it. He didn't say anything, and I didn't say anything. At the time I didn't wonder whether he was doing the same thing to my brother. I've asked my brother about it since, and he has said it didn't ever happen to him.

Then, while my father and sister were both still in hospital, I caught the measles. I can't imagine how hard that must have been for my poor mother. She already had so much going on. The priest suggested that he would look after me on the days when mum needed to go to the hospital. And that was when he started to come into the bedroom to abuse me. I remember he was very aggressive about it. Even though he was nice with everyone else, I felt his enormous aggression towards me whenever we were alone. It was the most terrible experience, and I felt that I was suffocating. I can't remember how many times it happened or how long it continued. I just remember being hurt and terrified.

The priest made it clear to me that I must never, ever tell anyone about what was happening. He said no one would believe me and my mother would be completely heartbroken if I said such things. He made me understand that if I ever told anyone the truth, I would be severely punished. I believed that if I ever revealed what had happened, there would be horrific consequences for me and for the people I loved. Looking back on these horrible experiences, I can only describe it as an insidious spell he put on me. He programmed me with fear and threats, and I was left with a paralysis that stopped me from speaking to anybody. Until recently I lived under that spell and unconsciously kept my life small and predictable so that I would never have to face the horrible consequences he scared me with. Breaking that spell has been hard and traumatic. It's only now, as I write this book, that I feel the spell has been truly broken. I'm now seventy, and I lived with that fear for more than sixty years.

Looking back now, I can see how the priest groomed our family in a classic, predictable way. We were poor and we needed support. Everyone in my family really loved this man. My father didn't know him well, because he was often in hospital. But everyone else in the family thought the priest was wonderful. He was funny and charming and had my family's trust.

As a young child, I had a lot of natural goodness inside me. Being good and innocent was my essential state and I feel it was a gift from God.

Looking back from my position of understanding and acceptance now, I feel the priest used me to not only satisfy his own misplaced sexual urges but also robbed me of my life force. He wanted my innocence and get rid of his own darkness. I see this sexual abuse as being driven by a satanic force. That which has no inner light seeks to rob the light of the innocent child. The tragic part of such abuse is that the dark force is insatiable and therefore the abuse was not a one-off event. In actual fact, sexual abuse implies that the person who pretends to be a representative of God on earth is the embodiment of darkness. The priest's outer veneer, his mask of a jolly, charming man of God, fell off quickly when he was alone with me. The energy exchange seems to be related to damage of the lower chakras. My life force got sucked out of me as a consequence of the abuse. His hidden evil agenda also destroyed my personal connection with God. How could a man who preached about God make me feel so horrible? I was left with a deep feeling of shame and guilt and a sense that I was flawed in fundamental ways. To the outside world it may have appeared as though nothing had changed: I was a polite, placid boy with good manners. But deep inside me, I was broken, lost my zest for life and began to think of myself as being bad beyond redemption.

Objective Witness: Story revealed

Majnun is slowly awaking to the memories of the childhood abuse he experienced. It took him years of difficult, painful, fragmented recall to piece his traumatic encounters together. Now you can see the source of anxiety, the reasons why Majnun always felt all this shame and lacked confidence. You can see that his pain was the reason why he had created such a small, predictable and controlled life. Leyla not only expanded his emotional and physical life but also accompanied him on his journey to Sufism and Islam that served as a spiritual holding for his awakening.

This world is a place of preparation where one is given many lessons and passes many tests. Ibn Arabi

New faith – Leyla

It was while I was living in Melbourne that a Sufi Sheikh visited Australia and I became very interested in his teachings. His talk was advertised in the Theosophical Bookshop in Melbourne, and I went along because I was keen to learn about something new. I learned a lot about Sufism from him as he gave weekly talks that introduced us to the many Sufis that had written on these topics over the centuries. He also mentioned the Dervish order in Konya in Turkey, and he showed us how to do the whirling as a means of getting into contact with God.

Every week we practised whirling after his teachings. In the beginning I became very dizzy because I didn't concentrate on repeating the name of God in my heart. He was extremely strict about the practice: he gave us a board with a nail in it, and we had to put our toes around the nail so we could whirl properly on the spot. If we didn't whirl correctly, we'd end up with very sore toes!

After a few months of learning from that British Sufi Sheikh, I began to ask myself what the meaning was of my life. My everyday existence lost its shine because apart from working, riding my motorbike and hanging out on the beach, it was spiritually pretty empty. After some soul searching, it took me two weeks to completely change my life. I sold everything I owned, resigned from my teaching job and started to travel. I was searching for the spiritual meaning I needed in my life, but at the time I didn't know what I was looking for and where to find it. I was twenty-eight years old, and I left my old life behind completely. Once I had either sold or given away all my possessions, I was left with only a small backpack that contained the most essential things I needed. I remember my shaky hands when I handed the keys to my St Kilda apartment to my landlord. These were the days before email, mobile phones or other easy means of communication. Neither I nor any of my friends had any idea where I was going or where I would end up. I was well aware that travelling by myself without leaving a trace was not without its dangers. But my spiritual longing was more acute than any possible second thoughts about the dangers involved. Once my key was handed in and I was virtually homeless, I set out without any destination in mind and bought a one-way ticket to Malaysia. From there, in each place, I just followed my inner GPS to find out where I should go next. I ended up travelling through Malaysia, Jordan, Israel and Egypt, using various means of transport and staying mostly in cheap hotels.

While I was travelling, I was mostly very careful. But I did take some risks that I realise now were unnecessary. I travelled through places with civil wars and all sorts of political tensions, but I was always divinely protected.

I decided to go to Jordan to see the desert castles and see where Lawrence of Arabia had travelled. I didn't realise then that I shouldn't go there by myself. It was actually very dangerous. A soldier said he needed to check me, and he ended up pointing his rifle at me and trying to rape me. In that moment I wasn't afraid of death at all. I said he could kill me if he wanted, but he couldn't break me, and I wasn't going to let him rape me. I got up slowly and walked away, expecting all the time that he would shoot me in the back. He didn't, and I think I was protected in that moment. God had plans for me and I needed to live.

When I was in Jerusalem, I stayed in the Arabic quarter that was under curfew. One night I woke up feeling hungry and decided to go out looking for food. Of course, I was breaking the curfew, and I had soldiers pointing machine guns at me from the rooftops. No one else was on the street. Just me, looking for a sandwich. As I was walking through the streets of the dark quarter, my steps echoed, and I half expected to be killed before having a meal. It seemed unfair to me that the Christian and Jewish quarters were alive and buzzing. Once I had eaten, I slowly walked back to my hotel hidden in the shadows of the old city. The soldiers with their machine guns were still on the roof staring at me in disbelief. I guess they weren't sure whether I was just naïve or stupid. I finally managed to get back to sleep.

When I was in Egypt, I stayed in a small hotel near the markets. I must have eaten something from the stalls and had terrible food poisoning. My room didn't have a telephone and for three days I was so sick I could not move or call out. I was basically rotting in my room without being able to get any help. Eventually I realised I either had to crawl down the stairs or I would die from dehydration by myself.

Everywhere I went on my travels, I visited the local mosques. They were beautiful places to sit – so cool, pleasant and soothing. I spent hours enjoying the quiet peace, admiring their artistic calligraphy and stained-glass windows inside these different mosques, all over the world. And the more I travelled, the more I started to realise that I was being led on a journey. There was a voice inside me saying 'do this', 'now do this'. I just followed the instructions, and I was always protected. Eventually I got the instruction 'go to thirty-three', but I had no idea what it meant. The number thirty-three meant nothing to me, and I didn't know where I was supposed to go. What is thirty-three?

I decided to go to Konya in Turkey, because that's where Mevlana Rumi is buried, the thirteenth century poet and master I'd learned about from the Sufi teacher in Melbourne. I wanted to pay my respects to Mevlana Rumi and see his tomb. And when I got to Konya, I discovered that its telephone area code is thirty-three! It was such a clear sign. This was where I was meant to go, but I hadn't realised it. In the following I recount my journey to Konya.

Visit to Konya, Turkey – Leyla

The road leading to Rumi's Tomb in Konya, Turkey, appeared spectacular to me in spite of my tiredness after the long bus trip. For so long I had dreamed about visiting his tomb to pay my respect to him. Jallaluddin Rumi lived in the 12th century, but his poetry and mystical teachings had kept me inspired in these last few years of soul-searching. However, arriving late at night in a town where I knew nobody, I had to first look after essential necessities like finding a room and some food before relaxing into the next step in my spiritual quest.

I enjoy travelling by myself. I love the freedom to follow my own inclinations on the spur of the moment. I can drop to a level of inner guidance that is harder to maintain when I have to accommodate the needs and wishes of a travel companion. But there are moments when the company of someone familiar is sorely missed. As I stand at the bus stop in Konya, watching all other travellers being picked up by their family or friends, I notice that little, lonely twinge in my heart. They know where they are going to sleep tonight. Someone has probably cooked a welcoming meal for them. The happy faces that greet them are nourishment for their souls. Moments like these are tainted by a nostalgic melancholy that only the solo traveller can understand. When you stand at a lonely bus stop on a cold winter's night and nobody cares where you are going and whether you have eaten by yourself, travelling shows its melancholy face. I have learned not to resist these moments, to allow myself some time for feeling sorry for myself because that is the fastest way to get back to my cheerful self.

The practicalities of putting on the backpack, grabbing my shabby grey plastic bags with various leftovers in them and walking down the street in search of a clean, safe hotel while ignoring the stares that inevitably follow me in such situations, quickly chase away my momentary sense of abandonment. After all, I chose to travel alone and, if I am honest, I'd rather have some lonely moments than a grumpy companion at my side. That night I did not have to walk far to find a suitable hotel where I could have a hot shower (quite a luxury in some places) and drop my backpack on an old rocking chair that had seen better days.

Personal safety has become a priority for me. I have learnt to first of all check all the locks of my room after some unpleasant surprises in other countries. Despite the added expense I also make sure that my room has a bathroom and toilet, so I don't have to walk down some half-lit corridor in the middle of the night. Once I have made sure that these two conditions are granted, I check the windows to see if the noise at night is bearable enough to sleep with an open window. Mind you, that first night in Konya was bitterly cold and I wasn't that keen on getting fresh air.

The trip from Istanbul had taken all day and my bones were a bit stiff from sitting that long. The beauty about Turkish buses is that they are inherently relaxing. The bus drivers welcome their guests with lemon water, which is squirted into each passenger's palms.

Bus stations are places of separation as well as reunion, and in Istanbul there were a number of people who farewelled their relatives or friends. The demonstrative emotionality that we are used to in Western countries, the kisses and hugs, the tears and heart-wrenching looks, these displays of the inner workings of human beings are missing in Turkey, where appropriate manners as prescribed by Islam. The religion not only regulates the public relations between husband and wife, but also, due to the trust put in the beneficent Almighty, people rely on seeing each other again if God wills. 'Insha'Allah', God willing, is a frequently used term, only outnumbered by 'merhaba' (hello) and 'hos geldiniz' (welcome).

Despite the controlled emotions that send the relatives and friends off on this twelve-hour trip, it seems to me that everyone is relieved when the bus finally departs. One last round by some young Turkish boys who sell pastries and bread, soft drinks and glasses of tea, and we are on our way. The comfort provided by the soft upholstery and the traditional Turkish music that plays quietly in the background is enhanced by the generally relaxed attitude of the travellers.

Having travelled on countless buses in numerous countries, I often found it difficult to relax because usually people talk incessantly. Egypt was one of those places where talking is one of many national sports. I have come to the conclusion that nations, the same as people, tend to be either rather talkative or rather silent. The Turkish mentality leans towards silence.

As soon as the bus rolls out of the hectic bus station, a quiet bubble starts to envelop the passengers. One can hear the clicking of prayer beads (tesbih) or the soft whisper of a grandmother and her grandchild, but despite these slight sound waves, a sea of silence pervades the bus. There is nothing to do and nothing much to say, which leaves me in a state of wonderful relaxation. Thoughts come and go as they please, but none stick around for too long because the underlying quiet shushes them away before too long. Nothing seems to leave much of a dent in the usual grooves of the brain. This is enough reason in itself to travel within Turkey on a bus.

My Western mind, being used to a constant chatter and internal commentary, finds it hard at first to just drop into this bubble of silence, but it does not take long before even my monkey brain gives into the softening effect of the peace that emanates from this collective unconscious. Every thought that tries to assert itself as an important wave soon loses its power and melts into the silencing ocean without much fuss. It leaves me free to admire the changing scenery without judgment or comment. What a relief to see it as it is, without my constant 'nice, average or ugly' subtitles.

When thoughts arise, they appear as air-filled bubbles that soon lose their outer form and then become air again. Not dissimilar to soap bubbles whose lifespan is limited. The trip does offer the opportunity to let scenes and experiences from the past few weeks and months pop up for revision, but obsessions about anything do not have any hold on me.

Sitting in the bus to Konya, I can digest my experiences and file them away in rhythm with the up and down movement of the smooth suspension. Why I am going to Konya is not altogether clear to me. Yes, I have been a great admirer of Rumi for many years and I do believe that paying respect to such rare individuals is worthy conduct. I am not expecting anything from this visit although I have wanted to see his tomb and mausoleum for a long time.

On a larger scale, however, it seems as if I am following an internal call that goes beyond respecting good manners. My experiences in the last few months have taught me not to question my instincts but to follow them with an open curiosity. I am sure that sooner or later I will know why I had to go to Konya. Right now, reasons and explanations lose their usual attraction.

My internal state of implicit trust gets slightly ruffled whenever the bus driver toots his horn to chase away a reckless guy on a motor roller who derives a sense of pleasure when he can block our way for more than ten minutes. I can almost feel his internal sense of invincibility with the accompanying adrenaline rush as he zigzags in front of the bus every time our driver wants to overtake him. The power of the little mouse challenging the elephant! Our driver seems to enjoy this harmless banter as a welcome interruption to his own train of thoughts that might move aimlessly like mine from one topic to another.

Welcome or not, the bus driver has to get us to our next destination within a determined time frame and, when his patience finally runs out, he decides to overtake the laughing youth in a simple display of strength, ready to push him off the road if need be. 'Crazy guy' one passenger comments and no-one is sure who is meant. But several of them agree 'evet, mejnun'. The young guy waves now from behind the bus and soon disappears in the distance, his short moment of glory still leaving a smile on his face.

And back we go to our velvety, dreamy peace. Our trip is interrupted a couple of times for refuelling, toilet stops and visits to roadside restaurants. We order kebabs, köfte, sandwiches and endless glasses of tea, usually sweetened with at least two extra-large cubes of sugar. The food always looks fresh and the cooking aromas lack the grease so typical for fast-food outlets in Western countries. I almost miss fish and chips, which are nothing but childhood association of long trips away from home. Here in the clean-tiled Turkish restaurants, the food looks as if it had just been cut by an old lady with a head scarf at the back of the kitchen. The yoghurt (obligatory for every good Turk) is enticing, and my stomach is grateful for my loading up on it at every stop. I also love the traditional Turkish Pide, a kind of mini pizza filled with vegetables, meat, eggs or cheese. By the time we arrive in Konya I have tried all varieties, washed down with either black or apple tea.

The simplicity and freshness of the food gives me a feeling of satisfaction without the full heaviness I am so accustomed to from roadside diners in Australia. There, the dim sims, sausage rolls, wedges or hot dogs inevitably result in regret ten minutes after consumption. While I sit in these neon-lit diners savouring Turkish tastes, I observe that many people use the break to perform their prayers. Many service stations and restaurants have little mosques attached to them, where the believers say their lunchtime and afternoon prayers in a summarised version as Islam permits the traveller to do. It is not just old ladies dressed in dark coats and scarves with crocheted edges who talk to God when the opportunity presents itself. The young and the old go to the mosque before joining the lunchtime queue. I admire the naturalness of their devotion and become intrigued by the faith that instils it in them.

Once our breaks are completed, we are back on the road again. I watch the mountainous curves that, once in a while, open the view to fields where donkeys lead their owners up worn paths. It seems as if women do most of the farming work, picking fruit and sometimes tobacco, which leaves their fingers sticky with a dark gooey substance. Babies are sometimes tied to their backs or put to sleep in the field amongst groups of women who are engaged in an initial form of sorting and packing. Maybe Turkish men are the ones who sell the produce at the markets, but in the fields, they shine through their absence. The rhythmic movement of the quiet bus soon wraps me in a relaxed blankness that disallows any indignation about gender equality or the lack thereof. These arrangements seem to work for them and who am I to judge.

I fall back into the common consensus trance that observes the happenings outside and inside the bus from a disengaged viewpoint. The day passes in slow motion with minor events blending into the relaxed whole. Towards the end of the day, the bus driver turns up the heater, which enhances the meditative atmosphere. Upon arrival in Konya, the cold air and the reality of life outside this protected comfort zone hits me with an unwelcome force. I have no desire to get off the bus. Torn away from my Turkish travel companions, I feel all the more left alone and cold when it is time to leave the comfort of the bus. Another chapter has been completed and I hope the real purpose of my visit to Konya will reveal itself soon.

After a warm dinner of more köfte and a restful sleep in my hotel room, I wake up to the call to prayer, which I hear coming from various mosque loudspeakers at around 6:30am. 'Allahu Akbar, Allahu Akbar' can be heard from all directions. I have read that the call to prayer in the morning says that prayer is better than sleep, but I am not sure on that particular morning if I entirely agree. Pulling the heavy feather doona further over my sleepy eyes, I cannot help but hear and listen to the musical invitations. I wonder how the inhabitants of this city, known for its devoted believers, feel about this call to prayer. How many will get out of bed and pray and how many will ignore their spiritual duty?

Coming from a country where we only hear church bells on Sundays at a decent time of the day and on special occasions, it seems strange at first to hear this call five times a day. However, it has grown on me over the past few weeks travelling through the Middle East. But nowhere has the call to prayer seemed as insistent as in Konya. I decide to get up, shower, and go out hunting for some breakfast. Many cafés are already open, offering Turkish bread, feta cheese, honey, olives and tea or coffee. The café I choose is full of Turkish men who have come back from the mosque to catch up with their friends. The cafe is filled with heavy cigarette smoke and questioning stares. I order my breakfast as if it were the most natural thing to do and begin to study the posters that display Quranic calligraphy and show Turkish seaside towns. The men's cigarettes irritate me more than their stares, but being aware that I am the one who is invading their territory, I try not to show my annoyance.

The warm Turkish bread, which I dip in grape jelly, and the strong black Turkish coffee chase away any remaining feelings of discomfort. In my limited Turkish I ask the waiter for direction to Rumi's tomb:

'Nerede …?'

'Just go straight along this road and then follow the signs. But if you want to visit Rumi, you first have to ask for permission from Konevi.'

'Konevi?' I wonder, 'Who is he? Some sort of gatekeeper?'

'No, there is an order to the visits, first it is Konevi, then Shams-I-Tabriz, then Rumi himself.'

Konevi was a student of the Great Sufi Sheikh Muhyiddin Ibn Arabi. It was Sadreddin who taught Maulana before he met Shams-I-Tabriz, who was his closest friend and main source of inspiration. 'Wow', I think to myself, 'did I miss that in the Lonely Planet Book or is this local Konya etiquette?'

'Well, where is the tomb of Konevi then?'

He gives me directions, but since they are quite complex, he asks another man in the café to guide me there. As many times before on my travels, I put my trust in a complete stranger and follow him through obscure streets and alleyways. It seems crazy to follow a man I don't know, especially since a couple of days earlier I had run into three German men who were travelling together because they were too scared to travel alone. Here I am, a Western woman following a Turkish man into the heart of old Konya. He could have led me anywhere, but my instinct has guided me for months and it feels perfectly safe to be in this situation now. The man says:

'If God wills it, the door to Konevi's tomb will be open and, if God doesn't will it, it'll be closed. Then you'll have to come back again tomorrow.'

'And if it's closed tomorrow?'

'Then you come back the next day.'

'And if it is closed the next day?'

'Then you come back the next day!'

I wonder how long this might go on for. He tells me that many people need to leave Konya before they ever get the chance to pay their respect to Konevi. In simple Turkish, interspersed with a few words in English, he tells me a bit more about Konevi who was the main force behind Rumi expressing his poems and teachings on paper.

Maybe it is because it is still early and cold that I am fortunate enough to find the door to the little mosque open that houses Konevi's tomb. My unknown travel guide is visibly happy for me and offers further explanations now that in his mind Allah has allowed me this visit. Apparently, Konevi used to perform his religious practices in a small cell next to the mosque where he could neither lie down nor sit comfortably. The cell is that small that I cannot even imagine a ten-year-old child being able to move in it. In this way Konevi ensured that he would not fall asleep in nights of vigil. The story goes that he would spend periods of forty days and nights at a time in this cell in an attempt to come closer to God. I marvel at such dedication. The simple mosque has a calming effect on me, and the cold does not seem quite as biting any more.

Over the last few weeks and months, travelling through the Middle East, I visited a number of places of worship and found most mosques were filled with calming energy. I remember sitting for hours in a big mosque in Amman, Jordan. The beauty of the calligraphy on the walls, the simple yet exquisite patterns on the carpet, the light and sunshine that filters in at all hours of the day, the immaculate ablution facilities, and the roundish shape of the mosque that promises archetypal holding, all attracted me again and again. I must have been a strange sight to the worshippers, this Western woman with a scarf clumsily wrapped around her head, sitting on the carpet waiting for nothing.

There are mosques of surreal beauty, others that are unbelievably simple and modest and many that were only built because a rich benefactor tried to elevate himself in the eyes of God. In my experience, a mosque is as good as the worshippers who pray in it. In Istanbul, for instance, I, together with thousands of other tourists, admired the Blue Mosque for its architectural grandeur. However, it was a tiny mosque that I stumbled across in the back streets between the university and the bookshops near the Grand Bazaar that attracted me the most. I felt instantly at home in it, sometimes slightly distracted by women who adjusted my clothing or scarf so I would fulfil the unspoken requirements of the Turkish-Muslim dress code. Women gave me their prayer beads with just a simple nod of the head that signalled 'here for you, may it help you' and went back to their own silent repetition of God's names.

In the middle of the Istanbul traffic noise, yellowish smog and incessant market cries, I would often find myself thinking back to this quiet female oasis. I am not even sure I ever saw any men there at all. If I did, they did not leave any impression. The women, mostly dressed in dark colours, who had probably interrupted their household chores or vegetable shopping, granted themselves a period of reprieve, in which they forgot their duties and focussed solely on communicating with God. I often thought back to my job as a teacher in Melbourne, where eating a bought sandwich in front of a computer was my pathetic attempt at a lunchtime break.

These women found a sense of peace and solace in bowing and prostrating either in unison with others or by themselves. Resting their foreheads onto the old purplish-red carpet, they seemed to become even more grounded. Peace settled over the worshippers. Sitting amongst them without the slightest discomfort about the physical closeness we all shared, I often felt a deep sense of primordial belonging without exchanging a word.

After a few days, I began to recognise some faces and felt happy when a woman gestured with her hand that there was space beside her that she would like me to occupy. But apart from this short acknowledgment of my existence, they quickly went back to clicking their prayer beads, silently reciting words that comforted their hearts. The cacophony of Istanbul instantly dropped away; it simply was no longer there because my attention was withdrawn from it. These moments of deep rest, of feeling that all will be well and right now, in this very moment, the world and I are at peace, meant a lot to me.

While I only visited the Blue Mosque once, I returned to the little nameless mosque at least a dozen times. The sincerity of the women reduced the threadbare carpet to an insignificant observation. Its atmosphere reminded me of a little chapel in Bethlehem, called the Milk Grotto, named thus because the Virgin Mary was said to have nursed Jesus on that spot. This chapel, with its knobbly wooden pews, attracted me more than the Church of Nativity, in which hundreds of pilgrims and tourists touched or kissed the place where Jesus was born. Maybe the touristy energy of haste and hunger for experiences has a homogenising effect on the place of attraction. Being pushed along by droves of people who chat, sweat and take photos usually does not leave much room for soaking up the original atmosphere of the place.

My nameless guide, now visibly pleased that God had deemed me worthy of keeping the door to Konevi's mosque open, is eager to make sure I also seek the pleasure of Shams-i-Tabriz. Before going to Rumi's mausoleum, called the 'Green Dome', I have to pay a visit to the memorial of Shams-i Tabriz as well because, as he states, if I didn't, 'Shams will be angry with you!' This second step of my tribute to Rumi also went smoothly and I began to wonder if the Turks had invented the 'closed door' myth to make Western travellers feel special. I guess I will never find out.

After paying my respect to Shams-i Tabriz, whose tomb did not leave much of an impression on me, I was keen to get to Rumi's resting place. His famous words echoed in my ears:

Come, whoever you are, come

You may be an infidel, a pagan or a fire-worshipper, come

Our brotherhood is not one of despair

Even though you have broken your vows a hundred times, come!

It is no wonder that such a mystic who died in 1273 has a universal appeal that reaches the hearts of followers of all religions. Rumi has become the best-selling poet in America more than 800 years after his death, which I think shows that truth can touch the human soul in a way that takes no note of time and space. Rumi's longing for love, simultaneously divine and human, and his utter vulnerability that yearns for peace brings him close to mere mortals like me who feel the same impulse but lack the eloquence to express it in beautiful verse.

Rumi removed all veils of protection from his heart, which allows me to go deeper into those layers of my own soul that I normally keep under control. His love for God, whether expressed in poetry, music or whirling, speaks through his uncompromising intensity. His humanity, so exquisitely articulated in his unconditional acceptance of people of all religious backgrounds, opens me up to previously unknown levels of appreciation and simplicity. It feels good to spend some hours exploring the museum that gives more insight into Rumi's life and work. And for me, it is particularly interesting to look at pictures of Sufi mystics (dervishes) turning in long white gowns, with arms held high, spinning around their own heart in an attempt to come closer to God. This dance, called Sema, is a symbol for the spiritual journey each individual follows as they increasingly abandon their ego and turn towards the truth.

During the past couple of years, I had practised this whirling in Melbourne under the direction of a Sufi Sheikh who had come out from England. He was a strict but kind task master. We had to practise on a wooden board, on which a long nail stood out. We had to put the nail between the big toe and the second toe of our naked foot to make sure we would turn around ourselves. Many times, my toes had hurt from the constant friction against the cold nail. I am not sure if the technique or the fear of it led to me learning the necessary stability very quickly.

When it was time to practise the turning in a group, moving around our own axle as well as the groups', I often had dizzy spells. How many times can one person spin around in circles before they become completely disoriented, I often wondered to myself. I kept persisting though, and I remember the moment when the dizziness stopped. It happened because I had made the intention to keep repeating God's name in my heart. My mind did not wander; I forgot to be self-conscious; I repeated the sacred name and abandoned my fear of the unpleasant dizzy feeling. The first time it worked I was very happy, simply to know it was possible. From then on, I could measure my sincerity and presence in how long it took before I became dizzy. The more distracted I was, the quicker I got the queasy feeling in my stomach.

Whenever I was not concerned about achieving something, when I just wanted to come closer to God for His sake, rather than my own, when I managed to keep focussing on nothing but His name, I could turn forever. Time would melt into eternity, my surroundings fully in my awareness but without any hold on my attention. I often had the feeling that in those moments I ceased to exist, and nothing could have been more pleasant. Getting out of my own way, becoming an instrument of devotion, cleansing my heart and aura of any unnecessary clutter was such freedom. I loved the lightness, the joy, the simplicity of just being.

My next step was that I did no longer experience the turning as a form of practice or doing, it seemed to become an expression of being. I wondered how I ever lived my life without this manifestation of my innermost core. As this shift happened, the talks that the Sheikh gave before the whirling took on another level of significance. Before that time, when dizziness was the order of the day, I had seen the talks as separate from the practice, not only because there was a distinction between non-dizzy and dizzy time but because I could relate the content to the personal experience of the whirling. Once I had broken through the barrier, I heard each word he said as descriptions of my own experiences. Theory and practice lost their distinction, personal experience of God replaced them on both counts.

Having had these experiences myself gave me a new pair of eyes through which I could examine the photos of the performances of the Mevlevi order. I decided there and then that I wanted to watch such a performance by 'real Turkish Sufis'. They say that intention is the first step in achieving one's dreams. When I walked back from Rumi's tomb, a Turkish carpet seller asked me if I wanted to buy a carpet. I replied: 'No, I am looking for Sufis.' He said: 'Come back tonight and I will teach you.'

He made sure I was put up by a young female piano teacher because he considered hotels to be dirty places. Every morning I had to tell him my dreams. During the day he told me Sufi stories and explained the deeper significance of Rumi's teachings. During the seventh night, I dreamed about guiding Muhammad's horse, Buraq. The carpet dealer said: 'You're ready'. I said: 'Ready for what?' He said: 'Don't ask, just follow'. We took a bus. Another 8-hour night ride to the mountains behind Manisa. That is where he introduced me to his Sheikh. I found out then that he had sent out the call to prayer across the world months beforehand. Obviously, I was one of those who had heard it.

Becoming a Sufi

The Sheikh invited me to become part of the Sufi group he taught. It's unusual for a single woman to be accepted into a Sufi group, but he offered to accept me and said I needed to start my prayers straight away. At first, I wasn't convinced. I thought I was a Buddhist, and I didn't want to be a Muslim. I didn't feel I was ready for that sort of change. But he said my reaction was typical. There was a resistance inside me that didn't want to submit to the rituals and practices of Islam. The sheikh told me that I would get used to the prayers. I felt very comfortable in the community and after a couple of days my teacher and his wife became like parents to me. In fact, my sheikh explained to me that he and his wife were my spiritual parents. My biological parents had given me my body, but it was his task to help me develop my soul.

Before I was accepted into the Sufi group, I had the typical prejudices about Islam of most Western women. I thought my freedom would be curtailed. I thought I wouldn't be able to travel by myself. I considered myself a free spirit, and I was used to taking all sorts of adventures by myself. Since then, I've learned I was completely wrong. They were nothing more than prejudices. If anything, I've gained more freedom as a result of Sufism.

I stayed in Manisa for a while in 1989, and eventually rang a good friend in Germany to talk about what I was going to do next. I had left Melbourne behind and wasn't keen to go back. She said that just five minutes before I called, a language institute had called her to ask whether I was available to do some teaching. That was another sign! I accepted the job immediately and went to Bremen in North Germany to teach. From Bremen I could make regular visits to Manisa to learn about Sufism.

From the beginning of my path with Sufism, I have found my experiences with it to be completely convincing. Every part of it made sense to me: the dreams, the visions, the feeling I was being led in a particular direction, the travel, the way I met my teacher. It took me some time to get used to the daily practice, with the five prayers every day and the fasting in Ramadan. But over time, the prayers and the fasting have become a wonderful support system for my internal experiences and soul development. It became clear to me very quickly that in Sufism I had found exactly what I was looking for: something that gave me a full inner life, a deeply spiritual life, and a rich human life. With Sufism, there is no contradiction between the inner life and the outer life.

Once I was accepted by my Sufi teacher, he became my teacher forever. He's now 94, and he still guides me. Even after he dies, he can still give me direction through dreams. They will find a new teacher for the group, but we will never lose the connection with the teacher who initiated us into the group.

Being a Western Sufi – Leyla

At first, I kept my Sufi path a complete secret. I was concerned that I'd be met with ridicule and judgement. When I did tell people, I felt they didn't understand what it meant to me and why it was so important.

My friends accepted the things that mattered to me – like me not drinking alcohol anymore and not eating pork. But I always felt it was a reluctant acceptance, rather than a deep appreciation.

At work I tend not to talk about it. It can be difficult if there are work social occasions, or if people don't understand why I'm not eating during Ramadan. I don't want to say I'm Muslim and I'm fasting, because the prejudice is so widespread.

Even today after all this time, I don't go out of my way to tell people I'm Muslim. I always wear a necklace that has an Allah sign on it, and sometimes people will see it and understand. I've had some students notice it and become very excited because so many university teachers don't understand the issues that young Muslim students face. They feel I have a special connection with them because I understand them.

I am strict with myself about keeping the prayer routine. I follow the pattern of prayer and make sure my prayers are said at the appropriate times. There's a shift in energy at the moment of prayer – a shift in the patterns of nature. The birds become quiet, because they're at prayer. Even cats behave differently. People who don't pray following the Islamic schedule are deaf to these changes. The changes are so subtle that most people miss them. But to me, the power that comes from the energy shift and from knowing the whole world is at prayer brings me strength and peace.

I'm stricter than Majnun in following the rhythms of the Islamic schedule. Majnun tends to be flexible about prayer times, while I prefer to do everything at the right time. I think that, for Majnun, it's a reaction to the rules and regulations of the Catholic Church. It doesn't really matter. It's the belief – the faith – that matters, not the outward following of rules and routine.

Objective Witness: A new path

So, Leyla was led on a journey of her own, following the call of her Sufi teacher. She begins her transformation from 'spiritual seeker' to Sufi pilgrim. She has found the path she is intended to follow. In Konya, Leyla found her true path in this life. Now, she needs to return to the Western world and learn how to live in it as a Sufi. As she discovers, living as a Sufi in the Western world is not always simple.

Embracing Islam – Majnun

In the following I will try to express the inner struggle that I experienced for more than two decades before realising that I could no longer serve as a Christian Brother. It culminated in me becoming a Sufi and Muslim. Outer events and inner turmoil went hand-in-hand for a long time. Since I grew up in a Catholic family and firmly believed in its practices and rituals, it even took a long time to begin the process of questioning why I could not relate to the familiar traditions anymore. What became obvious in hindsight was that I was drawn to the contemplative aspects of religion. I searched for inner contact with God. The rituals, such as receiving the body and blood of Jesus as in the Eucharist, left me feeling empty for a long time before I investigated why I didn't feel what others were experiencing or what I thought I should be feeling.

While some people question the faith, they were brought up in, I think it takes courage to contemplate leaving your faith and adopting another one, especially one that gets a bad press in Western countries. Looking back at the inner evaluation process I can say that my having been abused might have contributed to it being such a drawn-out process. People who have not been abused and have had a fairly stable upbringing seem to be less willing to accept circumstances that are not serving them. I, however, go to a default position of looking for the flaw in myself. I automatically move to the childhood default setting of "There is something wrong with me". That is why I searched for the lack of connectedness in myself. I didn't question the rituals of the Catholic Church but instead tried very hard to make them work for me.

It took decades before I accepted that I had to abandon that attempt and let go of the familiar faith. To this point I am happy for anyone who feels held by their faith, whatever that may be. Some of my family continue to follow the Catholic tradition and whenever we visit them, we are happy to go to church with them. I honour their dedication and am grateful that they practise what works for them. I am also grateful that they respect my conversion although they may not completely understand it.

The inner struggle I went through is reflected in the outer life events that I will recount in the following section. Conversion to another religion is the result of a soul-searching journey. Life seems to have contributed to prodding me in that direction.

For much of my time as a member of the Christian Brothers, I was a middle school teacher. One of the subjects I taught in the late seventies was comparative religion, which I had always found very interesting. I enjoyed showing the students slides of various religious holy sites to support their appreciation of different traditions and practices. My set of slides included beautiful images of significant Muslim sites, such as the Kaaba in Mecca and the Dome of the Rock in Jerusalem. I remember my strong physical reactions every time I showed these impressive images. I would experience a warm, tingling sensation through my body. It was strange and unexpected. It seemed as if I had a special connection with Mecca and the Muslim holy site in Jerusalem, even though I'd never been anywhere near these places. It made me curious.

I also became interested in mystical movements that were outside the normal Catholic tradition, such as Jungian depth psychology. I felt the Christian Brothers spirituality didn't offer enough soul nourishment for me, and I became very interested in reading the poetry of Rumi. A standout experience was when I attended a workshop with Jean Houston, who was invited to Sydney by the Catholic Church. She was a leading international educator, though not a Catholic. She spent the days teaching us about Rumi. My heart jumped! I experienced the power of the Sufi practice of dervish whirling, Rumi's poetry, and so much more. A door began to open for me, and I was ready to soak up everything she had to teach about the practices of Sufism. She offered me the soul food I had been longing for, which was a deep, very satisfying experience. I remember that a lot of attendees of the workshop didn't return after the first day because they felt her teachings weren't based enough on Catholic doctrine. In contrast, I was very grateful because my contemplative soul was being nourished.

While I was still part of the Christian Brothers, I started to study and practice breathwork, dance, drawing, and dreamwork and incorporated them into my spiritual practice. I was also involved in founding Mandorla, a house of prayer and spirituality for adults, under the auspices of the Christian Brothers, and that was very important to me.

Integrating unconventional practices into my personal life as a Christian Brother reflected my attempt to add a spiritual dimension to what became increasingly meaningless to me. Since I always felt that there was something wrong with me, I tried my hardest to fix myself. However, eventually I reached a point where I could no longer wholeheartedly practise Catholicism. I didn't go to confession for many years, and I stopped going to Mass except for special occasions. The rituals of Catholicism lost their significance for me. At a fundamental level I could see a lot of truth in the faith, but I felt it wasn't offering what I needed for my spiritual growth.

I became frustrated that the spirituality of Catholicism was rarely discussed. Instead, too much focus was centred on good behaviours, our need for forgiveness, and the value of service. I missed the relevance and significance of these ideals in terms of advancing on the spiritual path. The stories which were mostly told from an historical perspective left my heart and soul untouched. I was yearning for meaningfulness and guidance on how to come closer to God. The Christian Brothers spoke a lot about service and how selfless practice is a possible source of growth, but very little about its importance for spiritual advancement. I felt the Church had very little to say about how to mature as a human soul and how to build spiritual depth.

In my early years with the Christian Brothers, we had one ritual that really resonated with me on a spiritual level. Everything we did finished with 'Live, Jesus, in our hearts'. Whoever was leading the prayer would say that to finish it, and everyone would respond by saying 'forever'. The call and response of that prayer always meant a lot to me because it reminded me of a profound spiritual truth. However, while we said it at the end of a prayer or service as a signal of transition, it was too meaningful, in my view, to be used as such. I wanted to contemplate its significance for me personally. This is just one example of how I couldn't connect deeply with the spirituality of the Christian Brothers because their rituals lacked inner meaning.

In the early 1990s, when I was still a Christian Brother, I went to America to study the Depth Psychological Tradition, particularly of people like Carl Jung. I explored the relationship between the conscious and the unconscious and gained a master's degree from the Pacifica Graduate Institute in counselling psychology within the depth tradition. For my final thesis I examined Parsifal's adventures in search of the holy grail, which symbolises the journey towards the Self, the inner God image.

My struggles with my faith continued while I was in America. A few times I attended Mass at the local university near where I was living. I wanted to see how the Mass was offered to the young people there and I was curious to find out whether the ritual could still affect me. It didn't, and that's when I realised my faith in Catholicism was finished. While I didn't mind attending the Mass, I was a no longer affected by it in any way. Once I understood that, I decided it was absolutely essential for me to leave the Christian Brothers, even though it was a radical step.

I wrote to the Brothers in Australia, explaining that I had lost my faith and I needed to leave. I offered to return immediately, but they encouraged me to remain a member of the order until I finished my master's degree. Therefore, in 1993, I completed my degree and went through the steps of leaving the Christian Brothers. This meant that I had to write to Rome to outline my concerns and get dispensation of final vows. To help the transition, they gave me a small payout to start my new life.

After I left the Christian Brothers, I remained committed to my spiritual journey, but I didn't know at the time what that meant. My interest in the soul and in spiritual development didn't go away. I remained deeply interested in the expression of the human psyche. I read a lot of Rumi's poetry, and I was interested in Sufism. At that stage it was just an interest, nothing more.

I had a close friend who had been attending the Diamond Approach group, and she invited me to an introductory evening in Sydney. I went along out of curiosity, not because I thought it would offer anything in particular. At the session, the teacher talked about the Sufi idea that the spiritual journey is mirrored in the collection of honey by a bee. You gather the precious substance, learn about yourself and through an alchemical process convert the discovery into a new aspect of your soul.

I thought it was an interesting approach, so I signed up to study the Diamond Approach, which promised to give me more access to the inner make-up of my soul. You learn to be in the world but not of it, which is a very Sufi way of understanding the inner life. I wanted to live a rich inner life but still function in the world, and the Diamond Approach seemed to offer that.

I slowly became more interested in Sufism and Islam. I remember that I'd often catch a train that passed Auburn in Sydney where a mosque was being built, and I loved watching the building of the dome and the minarets. The water features at the front of the building and the coloured tiles caught my attention as the train drove past. When the mosque opened, I used to spend time sitting inside, watching people coming and going for their prayer. While I didn't join in, I was intrigued by the way they used their whole body in prayer. I continued to spend a lot of time contemplating Rumi's poetry and enjoyed reading some of the simpler Islamic texts, including those by Tarik Ramadan and Karen Armstrong. I clearly remember that I had a vivid, strongly moving dream on the Islamic symbol of the crescent moon and the star. This dream reverberated in me for some time.

When I met Leyla, I started to learn from her. She introduced me to a recording of the remembrance of God, called Zhikr, that reminded me of the power of the breath, which I knew from my years of working with breathwork at the Christian Brothers Mandorla Centre. Over time, Islam just made more and more sense. I formally converted in 1997 when Leyla and I were married Islamically and I was accepted into the Sufi group.

Although I'm not a theologian of Islam, I consider myself to be a devout Muslim. However, even today I find that many of the sermons at the mosque are too literal for me. When Muslim scholars insist on living like the Prophet centuries ago, I feel reminded of the Catholic rituals that lost meaning for my everyday world. I firmly believe that it is only the inner, mystical core of Islam that will ensure its relevance and survival. The rules and laws need to be connected to the inner communication with God. The minute they become divorced from the potential for spiritual advancement, I can't relate to them.

Deep value of ritual prayer – Majnun

For me, Islam is about my personal relationship with God. There's no intermediary; no hierarchical structure, no representative of God who is in charge of the rituals. It's just me involved in ritual practices that connect me with God.

I find spiritual nourishment in the five prayers throughout the day. The ritual washing (wudu), wakes me up and brings me back into my body. It is important to me that the prayers are preceded by the washing of the hands, forearms, face and feet. During the formal prayer, through the physical action of bowing and prostrating myself, I'm using my body to connect with the prayer. There is a moment, five times every day, where I can forget my worries, leave behind everything else that's going on, and concentrate on being aware of the presence of God, who is most gracious, most merciful. It's a practice that works for me and makes me deeply content. The Islamic prayer is fully embodied and the sequence of the movements, which culminate in the surrender to God by prostrating, make sense to me. The words that are recited internally go hand-in hand with each specific posture. At one moment there is an intimate conversation between God and the believer, which always reminds me of the direct contact that is possible. The combination of internal recitation, the postures and movements, the blessings that are expressed towards all the prophets, going back to Abraham- these all appear to me as a well-rounded process. I also appreciate that the ritual prayer can be performed anywhere, alone or with others. All I need is a clean surface, be sand, a towel, or a small mat, to perform my prayer, regardless of where I am. This ease, the inclusion of our Jewish and Christian 'people of the book', the directness of the contact, the integration of body and mind, all of these simple expressions of the many layers of spiritual practice five times a day have convinced me of the effectiveness of the Muslim prayer.

The Islamic tradition of five prayers each day has a beautiful naturalness to it. The timing of the prayers is connected to the movement of the sun, which means the cycles of prayer and nature are intimately intertwined. The natural cycles and rhythms of Islam have been critical to my recovery. Through the rhythm of the daily prayers, I have experienced greater meaning in my life. While the prayer times change with the movement of the sun, the month of Ramadan is based on the movement of the moon. It involves a month of fasting during the day, which can be quite challenging when Ramadan falls in the summer months as we might not eat or drink for 17 hours. Fasting is easier in the winter time. That is why it makes sense to me that Ramadan moves forward every year so that every Muslim can experience it differently throughout their lifetime. Fasting has deepened and strengthened my capacity for self-awareness and self-regulation. My inner psychological structures were damaged by the abuse I experienced, and these Islamic practices have supported me internally. I can see now that abuse can interfere with the development of healthy ego structures, the setting of boundaries and self-supporting attitudes and behaviours. In my case, the abuse resulted in rigid ego structures that compensated for the disorientation I experienced. The Islamic practices have given me a structure that is flexible, natural and at the same time solid. Like a reed that can bend with the wind, the fact that the next prayer will be called, the next month of Ramadan will surely come, regardless of my inner turmoil, this knowledge has given me a sense of safety and security that was shattered by the abuse.

Objective Witness: Powerful prayer

The flexible reliability of the embodied Islamic prayer gives Majnun the foundation he needs to come to terms with his disorienting experiences of abuse. The harmonious combination of physical movement and mindful recitation offers him stability, peace and calm focus. It teaches him patience and strength, which he needs to remember, accept and ultimately integrate his trauma.

The moment you accept the troubles you've been given;
the door will open. Rumi

Gradual Expansion – Majnun

In 1999, I applied for a leadership position at an Islamic Kindergarten to Year 12 school in Sydney. This was a huge decision for me. I had left teaching at the end of 1981.

By the early 1980s, I had lost my confidence in the classroom and believed that I wasn't able to effectively teach teenagers. Instead, I focussed on offering adults alternative ways of connecting with and nurturing their inner lives by working in a spiritual centre called Mandorla. There we integrated many different approaches, such as, breathwork, dance, meditation, journaling, and dreamwork.

Once I had completed my Master's Degree in Counselling Psychology and had left the Christian Brothers, I focused on building my counselling practice in Sydney. I can see now that my capacity as a counsellor was limited at that time because I had not yet become aware of my own story of abuse. In some mysterious way Leyla must have felt that counselling was not allowing me to live my full potential. I was working from home, saw people in my nicely set up room and fundamentally kept my life safe and small.

By the late 1990s, I was ready to expand my circle of influence. Leyla could see my leadership potential and she encouraged me to apply for a position as deputy principal at an Islamic school in Sydney. Although the prospect was daunting, I learned very early in our relationship that it's worthwhile listening to her because she has such good intuition.

I was challenged by leaving my small world of counselling from home, moving into an Islamic system, and leading older students and a group of teachers. However, this push into the deep end was what I needed to realise that I could swim in unchartered oceans.

Challenging roles

We eventually began to feel that Sydney was getting too crowded and we increasingly became irritated by the big city lifestyle with constant traffic jams. On advice of a psychic, we spent time on a holiday in Adelaide, which people often describe as a large country town. We both loved it from Day 1 and decided it would be a good place for us to live. The only problem was that it was shortly after I had accepted the position at the Islamic school in Sydney.

There was only one Islamic school in Adelaide, and at the time it only went to Year 3. They advertised for a new principal, and they were seeking someone who could expand the school to Year 12. I called them and talked about my experience, and they encouraged me to apply. After being offered the principal's position, we moved to Adelaide in January 2000. Leyla left her job at the University of Sydney to set up a business teaching English test preparation online. Her business was transportable, which meant the move was relatively straightforward.

I had so much to learn about how to expand a school. I feel now that it was a wonderful opportunity for me to leave my familiar self-identification as being small and ineffective behind and mature in lockstep with the school. In the beginning, the Islamic College was an early years' primary school with around 60 students. In my first year, I taught Year 4 part-time while also working as the principal. I thoroughly enjoyed having an opportunity to work closely with children again. During my ten years in Adelaide, I developed the school into an all-ages school (Kindergarten to Year 12) with around 600 students. The growth involved a major building program and refurbishment of existing facilities. My biggest challenge was to juggle the needs of the college board with the needs of staff and students. I saw it as my job to engage an effective culture of teaching and learning, without getting caught up in the more political, organisational issues. The expansion of the school forced me to build my strength and resilience. I enjoyed carrying the responsibility of leading the educational direction and working with the architect to see plans turn into buildings. In hindsight I needed the practical experience of establishing new structures and facilities. The outer growth of the school went hand in hand with my inner evolution. It is hard to think of yourself as small and weak when hundreds of people look to you for guidance and direction.

We thoroughly enjoyed living in Adelaide. The Central Market, the beautiful beaches, the peaceful pace and the sense of quiet sophistication soothed our nerves after noisy Sydney. Therefore, we decided to build our own home. For the first time in our lives, we were responsible for a home loan. This was a huge expansion for someone who had lived a very modest, protected life as a Christian Brother. Leyla took great pleasure in designing the house according to Feng Shui principles. She loves big spaces that are not cluttered with unnecessary dust collectors. We were like little children when the house was being built and we could see the progress. Her creativity and unconventional approach meant we had huge rocks delivered from the local quarry that we then cut to lay the outside area. Leyla also managed to find good quality tiles for the pool at a cheap price. This way she could fulfill her dream of a pool that looked out onto the ocean. The house we built turned into a sanctuary for both of us that offered us respite from the many challenges the school's rapid growth posed. We could not know at that time that it would also become a hospice for Leyla's brother.

Objective Witness: Growing confidence

Even though Majnun feels small and safe in routine, his soul is telling him that it's time to expand his horizons. His self-image is changing as he ventures into a bigger world. He is beginning to believe that he can contribute as a leader in education. He is ready to take more risks, which despite being scary, allow him to experience more joy.

Move to Adelaide – Leyla

Not long after we got together, we wondered about leaving Sydney and yet had no idea where we should go.

We went together for a reading with an astrocartographer and explained to him that we were looking for a place to settle down. He suggested Adelaide and we decided to go there for a week's holiday. To our surprise, we loved it there straight away. Just before we were due to return to Sydney, we were standing on the jetty at Brighton Beach, looking towards the lighthouse on the hill to our right. We both agreed in that moment that we would like to live on that hill in Adelaide.

Once back in Sydney, we were delighted to find out that Majnun was offered the principal's job with the Islamic school in Adelaide. Packing up and getting ready to move was easy because we were so much looking forward to starting a new chapter in our lives. After a while we started to look for a house to buy and, of course, the first place we were magnetically drawn to was that suburb on the hill. We had so much trouble finding something, and for a while we thought the guidance about that suburb wasn't going to work out. But one day I found a tiny advertisement in the local newspaper about some land being subdivided. It was exactly the right spot for us. It was a house and land package that was advertised, and we had to negotiate hard about the type of house we wanted to design. We also struggled to get a home loan. But eventually it all came together, and we were able to build the house on the spot we'd imagined while standing on the jetty. It was a great moment when we were handed the keys and could complete the interior decorations.

Objective Witness: Guided creativity

Leaving noise but also important friends and familiar surroundings behind in Sydney and starting a new life together in Adelaide allowed them to grow in unexpected ways. While Majnun took on the challenges of a new position of responsibility, Leyla could express her creativity by developing her business and designing their house on the hill. Her interest in energy work, Reiki and Feng Shui meant she could translate these teachings into practical applications. Building a house from scratch allowed her to be playful and to express her unconventional approach to design, colours, and materials. The background canvas was prepared for their personal and spiritual developments.

Moving on spiritually – Majnun

In 2002, about two years after we moved to Adelaide, I lost interest in the Diamond Approach and decided to stop travelling to Sydney for retreats. For me, the teacher didn't explain things well enough and I could see that she didn't cherish Leyla as a student, who was already studying to become a Diamond Approach teacher.

Apart from being upset by the professional jealously that was directed against Leyla, I felt that I was not getting very far in my own process. It seemed to me that my teacher was not equipped to deal with my damaged ego structures, and I had to discover a lot more about myself. It had taken a few years for my confidence in the teacher to drop. As with the Christian Brothers, I finally realised that it was time to leave the school.

Spiritual reorientation– Leyla

I got tremendous value from studying the Diamond Approach. In 1997, I started to study to be a Diamond Approach teacher, which involved travelling to the United States a few times a year for training. When you're doing the teacher training, you need to remain part of a local group. That's why I continued with the Sydney group after Majnun left in 2002.

For some time, I travelled from Adelaide to workshops in Sydney. But gradually my enthusiasm for the workshops died away. The last time I went to Sydney, I got to the conference centre where the workshop was to be held, and I couldn't make myself go inside. I phoned Majnun and said I was stuck outside the building, unable to go in and I didn't know what to do. We eventually agreed that I should go home to Adelaide, and Majnun telephoned to say I wasn't well.

For a time, I joined a San Francisco group so I could continue with my teacher training. I kept at it until 2006, when I realised that I needed to move on. By the time I finished with the Diamond Approach I had almost completed my training. I learned a lot about psychological therapy and how to help people with their spiritual journeys. I only finished with the Diamond Approach because my brother Guido moved to Adelaide and he was very ill with cancer. I needed to focus on looking after him.

In the years after leaving the teacher training, I became increasingly concerned about some aspects of the organisation that seemed to lack transparency. Our Sufi teacher had never approved of it, because he believes in the power of devotional practices. Years later, when I was doing my PhD research on Ibn Arabi, I discovered some similarities between his Sufi teachings and those of the Diamond Approach. I still value the fact that the Diamond Approach has made some ancient teachings accessible to Western audiences. However, I could no longer whole-heartedly remain in a school that did not allow me to voice my concerns. I will remain grateful for many years of valuable spiritual teachings that have helped me to discover some of my ego patterns. I also still refer to the books that the founder has published. I guess I have never been good as a follower of a group.

Objective Witness: The next step

The time was right for Leyla and Majnun to part ways with the Diamond Approach and focus on walking their own path. The Diamond Approach had taught them a lot and had served them well. Leyla began to study again the ancient writings of Ibn Arabi, which resonated with the guidance of her Sufi teacher. Being on their own path further built their inner strength and helped them prepare to deal with new challenges.

Personal development – Majnun

I'm a different now to the person I was in 1994. I've been on a long, difficult and sometimes traumatic journey of self-discovery and inner healing. Before, I was anxious and lacking in confidence. While I could function in everyday life, I also kept my circle of influence small and safe. Now I feel that my life has greater purpose because I've come to terms with what happened to me when I was younger. I've accepted it and now I'm moving forward.

I've always been a person who finds security in routine. Being a member of the Christian Brothers, my life was all about routine and order. Even after I left them, my life was pretty boring, almost robotic. I think the routine was my way of protecting myself.

Life with Leyla is completely different from the routines I developed for myself. My daily existence with her is much more alive and spontaneous. We've made difficult, life-changing decisions together. We've done things I would never have considered possible for myself, such as travelling, having adventures and working overseas. I've also gained more confidence through understanding the abuse I experienced and talking about it openly.

I'm convinced that Leyla could see potential in me right from the beginning, which I was not aware of myself. Even early on, she would say 'there's more to you'. Looking back, I realise that other people saw potential in me, too, but I didn't know how to listen to them, and they weren't in a position to help. For example, when I was first teaching as a Christian Brother in Canberra, my principal saw my potential. He told me I had a great future as a school leader, and he transferred me from the primary school to teach in the secondary school. In addition, he promoted me to being the acting middle school principal although I didn't believe I could be a leader.

Sometimes I think I lived inside a self-contained capsule until I met Leyla. She helped me to recognise the capsule, which I didn't even know was there. She helped me to break it and truly enter the world for the first time. Even now, when we're apart I slip back into my simple routines. For instance, when I'm in Perth and Leyla is in Frankfurt, I fall into the routine of work, prayer, walking the dog and living a very simple life. Routine still makes me feel safe, but I don't think it's good for me. If it goes on for too long, it depresses me too much.

Life is a balance of holding on and letting go. Rumi

Liberating struggles– Leyla

In late 2015, we realised that Majnun's work opportunities in Germany were coming to an end because of strict rules regarding retirement. Therefore, we started to consider a return to Australia.

By 2015, Majnun had become aware of the childhood abuse and returning to Australia would enable him to work and give him a secure environment in which to come to terms with what he had learned. Also, retirement was not a realistic option for us because Majnun's twenty-eight years as a Christian Brother and my prolonged studies and casual jobs have left us both at a disadvantage in terms of retirement savings. This was when Majnun applied for the position of principal at an Islamic school in Perth. Being in Australia allowed Majnun to seek the help of a trauma specialist who not only understood his experiences but was also experienced in working with the effects of abuse.

For me Perth was more than difficult. I had only one friend, could not find satisfying, reliable work and suffered terribly from social isolation and meaninglessness. It was important to be there for Majnun but for me it was a torturous experience of confinement. Perth is not a city that satisfies my desire for adventure. While it is naturally very beautiful and its beaches and blue skies are outstanding, in terms of fulfilling my personal potential I felt at a loss. I tried to integrate by teaching a bit at the university, attending French courses and walking my dog. But overall, living in Perth has been very difficult for me, and if it hadn't been for Majnun, I would have left after a few months of giving it my best.

Objective Witness: Growth through struggles

Accepting positions in school leadership further developed Majnun's inner strength. In Adelaide, the challenges he encountered in growing the school prepared him for the tough lessons ahead when he moved to Germany. Even though he faced internal struggles and constant anxiety, his inner strength was growing. After his time in Germany, the school in Perth gave Majnun an opportunity to work as a highly effective leader.

Speaking out – Majnun

Sexual abuse can remain covered up for a number of reasons. The power distance between the perpetrator and the victim means that the crime can stay hidden for a long time. If a criminal act occurs between two equals, the victim is more likely to seek justice. However, the high social standing of a member of a religious order, which for me was also the representative of God on earth, meant that I was the one who had neither power nor credibility. The priest silenced me by making me believe terrible things would happen if I ever spoke to anyone about what had occurred. He was so threatening that I eventually buried the abuse deep within myself and couldn't remember or name it for almost sixty years.

The grooming that happens in cases of sexual abuse is a deliberate act of disarming parents by gaining their trust. At the time of the abuse, my parents were struggling on many fronts: my father and my sister were in hospital and we were very poor. The priest used this situation to such an extent that he could act on his plans. He abused me sexually and I dissociated as a consequence. I had no conscious access to those terrifying traumatic experiences. I was left petrified and all I could sense was that I must have committed a sexual mortal sin. Now that my memories have become more conscious, I feel sorry for that little child who was so horrified that it had only one way of coping with the experience, namely by dissociating from the body it was happening to. The priest was a master manipulator. He planned, committed and covered up the crime.

Moving to Germany rattled my familiar ways of keeping my life small, safe and predictable. The lack of familiarity opened up files in my memory bank that had been stored away for decades. When I first started to remember my abuse, I realised just how powerfully the priest had intimidated me into silence. I spent a long time not wanting to do anything about it. A part of me wanted to deal with it internally and then move on. However, eventually I realised that this would be another form of agreeing to the silence. It took a long time before I was ready to consider addressing the abuse with relevant church authorities. I wanted to experience true healing. Since the sexual abuse was the most significant part of my childhood, which influenced everything I did in future years, it deserved me speaking out. I therefore decided to contact Broken Rights, an Australian organisation for survivors of sexual abuse. They in turn directed me to an Australian law firm.

After I started to respond to requests for documents by the lawyers, I became excessively anxious. I'd wake during the night with an overwhelming fear that something terrible was about to happen to Leyla. It didn't make any sense at all, because it was an anxiety about Leyla, not about me and what I was doing. I didn't connect it with preparing impact statements that documented the abuse. I became so frightened that I even wondered whether she was sick and needed a medical check-up.

We used our process of inquiry to explore my anxiety and eventually we realised that it was linked to the way the priest had terrified me into silence. I had obviously internalised his threats and was convinced that serious harm would happen to the people I loved if I ever spoke about the abuse. All those years later his scare tactics still had a hold over me.

The anxiety was very difficult to shake. Throughout the legal action about the sexual abuse, every time I attended a meeting or wrote something about the case, I experienced an overwhelming fear that something terrible would happen. The priest's threats had programmed my nervous system and I had unconsciously accepted my frightened self as being my true nature.

Once I understood the origins of my anxiety, I worked consciously to reduce it. I gradually improved my ability to control it, for instance, by using Emotional Freedom Technique. This is a process of tapping that reduces the power and intensity of negative feelings and creates more capacity in me to be present. I learnt it from my trauma specialist, Chris Semmens. He supported me in dealing with difficult situations without dissociating, which was my normal way of handling situations. These days, I find that I can talk about the abuse without the fear or the physical reactions that would have stopped me in the past.

Today, I have a fundamental sense of myself that doesn't get shaken easily. I might still wake up anxious or be afraid in situations that make me feel the world is not safe, however, knowing now that this is not all of who I am, means that I can cope with it better.

Returning to Australia in 2016 and working in an Islamic schooling environment supported my healing process. Being offered the position of principal was a gift from God. When I joined the school in Perth, I took on the Islamic name Ridhwan, which means totally satisfied, fulfilled, contented. Ridhwan is the angel to paradise and taking on the name was like creating a psychic presence around myself that would actively support me. It helped me access the quality of contentment as I continued the journey of understanding, accepting and integrating further layers of my abuse.

Abuse or soul exchange – Leyla

We worked with a shaman in Germany who helped us understand that abuse often involves a soul exchange. The person who perpetrates the abuse has bad intentions and is often driven by negative forces.

The way we met our shaman was a typical example of the surprises that life can offer. I was teaching in Germany and spent a lot of time with my father, who was very unwell. One day there was a stand in the hospital where complimentary healing modalities were displayed. Being a Reiki Master myself I approached another Reiki practitioner and told her that my own capacities were not powerful enough to heal my father. She said that she only knew one person who could possibly assist and gave me the contact details of a shaman. The recommended shaman had an unusual surname, which was the same as a student's name in my language class. Yes, it was meant to be. The shaman who helped us so much was the mother of my student. She helped my father greatly, as you saw in my story about transitions. I will forever be grateful for how she healed my father emotionally so he could die peacefully. In the process we became friends and in real terms, I see her as my soul sister from Cameroon.

Majnun and I then consulted her to see if she could also assist Majnun. She saw psychically that the priest who had abused him fed energetically off Majnun's innocent soul. We are all energy expressing ourselves in physical bodies walking and talking on earth. Energy exchange can easily be observed when two people meet. In Majnun's case the priest used his power to rob him off his innocence while passing onto him his negative soul aspects. One could describe it as being fundamentally satanic because a child trusts an adult implicitly. To abuse this trust, physically hurt the child and then terrify them in case they reveal it, is nothing but acts committed by a devilish force.

When victims start to remember their abuse, they awaken all sort of negative forces and obstacles appear that make moving forward difficult. We believe all the things Majnun experienced – the prostate cancer, the employment difficulties in Germany, and trouble with his back – they're all negative forces we've had to deal with on the journey. It seems as if distractions appear that might be thrown up by the unconscious to avoid the painful memories.

The shaman showed us that the feelings of shame, guilt and sinfulness that Majnun carried all his life were misplaced in this process of soul exchange. It was the priest who should have been ashamed, feeling guilty and owning up to his sin. She took Majnun through a process of letter writing, various healing rituals to alleviate his burden. For me it was touching to not only learn more about the effects of abuse but to witness his sincere attempts to overcome them. I had to go through my own feelings of rage and anger against this priest, which I preferred to call 'the monster' because he doesn't deserve to be named. His crime not only caused tremendous pain and hurt for my husband but has also impacted my life because many times Majnun's lack of confidence has meant that I had to take over in situations that frightened him. A good example for my anger is that this monster's grave is not far from where we currently live. I have had fantasies of taking a spray can and writing in big letters 'paedophile' on the tombstone that commemorates his existence on earth. I have never acted on these fantasies because ultimately, I prefer to leave justice to God. I also see more benefit in transforming my anger instead of acting it out. But as the partner of a sexual abuse victim, I know that those who love the victim also bear the consequences of this crime.

Objective Witness: Enter hope

We thought Majnun was placid and quiet, but in reality, he was living through trauma and shock. Deep fear impacts a person's nervous system. It changes the way they relate to the world. Reducing fear requires effort and work – something that Majnun understands only too well. He is now well on the journey away from the small, weak boy he was and decides it's time to seek redress and justice. Even though he's scared, he's determined.

Leyla also had to dig deep in this process. From the beginning she always saw Majnun's potential and wanted him to live it. The insights offered by the shaman helped her understand why Majnun's anxiety persisted. She had to work through her own feelings of frustration, anger and helplessness while not missing a beat in accompanying him on his journey. The fact that the perfect support people appeared in the right moments shows that those two are not walking alone in the wilderness of difficult emotions.

Why do you stay in prison when the door is so wide open? Rumi

Institutional shadow – Majnun

If you'd asked me thirty years ago about my experience at a Christian Brothers high school in Brisbane, I would have said it was as good as could be expected. I wasn't happy at school, but I always assumed that my unhappiness was linked to my own feelings of insecurity and lack of confidence, not linked to anything about the school.

When I attended a professional development program for primary school teachers offered by Early Life Foundations in early 2018, I was shocked to recognise that my high school experiences amounted to having been abused.

I'd like to share my experience of seeking redress from the Christian Brothers regarding the physical and emotional abuse I experienced at school. In mid-2018, I contacted the Executive Officer of the Christian Brothers Professional Standards Office to make a formal complaint about my experiences in school. He put me in contact with a lawyer, who proposed a pastoral meeting to discuss my complaint.

The lawyer prepared me for the meeting, which was to involve me, Leyla, our lawyer, a Christian Brother, and a lawyer representing the Christian Brothers. My lawyer urged me to share my personal story about the destructive experiences I had suffered.

On the day of the pastoral meeting, Leyla and I arrived early to make sure we knew exactly where the meeting would be held. We filled in time by visiting the Catholic Cathedral opposite the meeting space. It was our first visit to the Cathedral, which was beautiful – silent, spacious and light-filled. We left the Cathedral feeling very positive about the forthcoming meeting.

In contrast to this uplifting atmosphere in the Cathedral, the meeting room was stuffy and stale. I drew my strength from Leyla, who sat to my left. I had provided them with the following statement:

I was at school in Brisbane, in Year 8, a Scholarship year in

Queensland. It was 1961. I have never forgotten the following incident:

The whole class of boys was lined up around the wall on the last day of Term 1. We were being assigned our new seating arrangement for the next Term. The atmosphere was serious. When it came to me, my teacher a Christian Brother, said in a very measured, deliberate, threatening, nasty tone 'Majnun, I am going to put so much pressure on you that you will leave by the end of next term'. I was the only student who was singled out like this. No one else was spoken to in this way.

I felt completely stunned and numb. I did not know why he spoke to me in this way. I felt painfully humiliated in front of the other boys. I didn't know what I had done wrong or why I deserved this public threat.

I was terrified and very scared. I was mortified in front of the class and immediately looked for the mistake in myself and thought there was something very wrong with me. I went blank and wanted to disappear.

During the holiday break I was very worried and did not know how to face school. After long soul searching, I went back to school feeling very scared. His verbal attacks on me had a profound effect on my self-confidence and self-esteem. Every morning I experienced high levels of anxiety on the way to school. I wished I did not have to go to school anymore.

Up to that point in time, I was regularly strapped on the hands by the Brother. He used a leather strap. He always hit me with all his force. However, in Term 2 after the incident I just described, I experienced his brutality in a terrible way – he was completely out of control. I received the most straps before recess (15 straps) of anyone in the class. He felt justified in being brutal that day because, according to him, I did not do well enough in my tests. He used any excuse to strap me. I remember that it happened in Term 2 because it was winter, and it all happened in the morning before recess and it hurt terribly. I have images of him being in an uncontrollable fury, red faced, angry and brutally hitting me with as much power as he could. I had the stuffing knocked out of me! I was literally in a daze, a very scared and frightened boy. I realise now that each time this happened, I dissociated.

In this teacher's class, I always dreaded going to school and into class. I never ever felt safe, secure or comfortable. I always felt so scared during the school day and anxious that I might make a mistake and get a belting or be verbally attacked. I was terrified of having to go to the chalkboard and do a maths solution or be asked to answer a question. My whole nervous system was stretched to the max. I was very, very anxious. I went inward, within myself, withdrawn, depressed, and school became a nightmare.

I felt completely vulnerable, sharing this personal, authentic story. I expected a warm, supportive response, appropriate to a pastoral meeting. However, the Christian Brother said that many Brothers in the 1960s were hard men. He attempted to normalise the abuse I'd received and said that most students just 'rode with the punishments', ignoring the fact that it was me who had been singled out. No other student in my class had received the same treatment.

In hindsight, I consider his response as cold hearted and lacking in empathy. It added insult to injury. For many weeks after the pastoral meeting, I had flashbacks, unwanted thoughts, disturbed sleep, anxiety, depression and an even stronger feeling that something must be wrong with me. Instead of receiving an apology, I walked away feeling suicidal. After a while, with Leyla's support, I eventually gathered my strength and ended up writing directly to the Executive Officer about the negative experience of the pastoral meeting.

This ongoing abuse at school has had long-lasting effects on me and influenced every aspect of my work. It has made me uncomfortable in learning environments at university and in professional development situations. I have also felt extremely uneasy about asking questions or speaking out in groups. It is interesting that my career choices led me to teaching – not just once with the Christian Brothers, but also in Germany and in Islamic schooling – when it was a teacher who created so much difficulty for me. I wanted to make sure that my students would never experience the trauma that I was subjected to.

Going through the formal process to seek recognition and compensation for trauma is something that no one would take on lightly. Even though I knew it would be difficult, I decided to go ahead because it seemed important for my development. I felt that formal recognition would give me a sense of closure and contribute to my healing. However, nothing prepared me for the traumatic experience of reliving the abuse, directly confronting the institutional abuse of the process and having to fight for justice. But with Leyla by my side, I was able to walk through it and emerge as a better person, more in touch with my strength and determination and more at peace with myself.

Objective Witness: Complex consequences

The abuse Majnun experienced was complex and multifaceted. Was there a pattern emerging? Majnun was the prime target for a bully – nervous, quiet and withdrawn. Abuse has long-lasting effects that stay with people throughout their lifetime. Majnun's growing strength and willingness to deal with his early trauma were challenged by the pastoral meeting. Instead of being a healing experience, it threatened to retraumatise. But Majnun would not be stopped. His self-image and confidence grew as he continued with his journey of healing. He learned to trust his inner strength. He always trusted Leyla's unwavering support. As the journey of healing progressed, Majnun became more of the person he was meant to be.

Companionship – Leyla

I'm not the same person now that I was when I met Majnun in 1994. I've become more multifaceted and thoughtful. We've been through a lot together, and I'm at peace with it.

When I met Majnun, I didn't have a care in the world. I lived my life for enjoyment and fun, always up for adventures, and I loved to go to unfamiliar places and take risks. I was what you'd call a free spirit.

Back then, I enjoyed discovering new countries and cities. At times when things went wrong – like the time I drove across the Nullarbor Desert and didn't have enough spare tyres – I felt peaceful and prepared to die. I've never felt afraid of death. When it's my time, it's my time.

I'm also conscious of how much Majnun has changed. He used to be such a scared little mouse, always terrified that something bad would happen. He believed that he couldn't cope in new situations. His good manners and calm exterior hid how he was feeling inside. He's so much stronger now.

Majnun and I didn't ever feel our path included having children together. I was in my mid-thirties when we met, and Majnun was already in his late forties. I felt that I'd done all the mothering I needed to do, looking after my younger brothers when I was a teenager. I also knew I wanted more freedom than would be possible with young children. Having children was never really something we considered.

Facing reality can be hard. Many people run away from it – through addiction, or depression, or refusing to explore what happened to them.

Majnun and I have made an enormous effort to face reality and the consequences of the abuse he experienced. We've talked about it, inquired into it, put our faith in God, practised rituals and sought professional help. We've also been through all the formal processes of bringing claims against the perpetrators. But once you've faced reality, you can't stay there. If you do, you'll have a miserable life. You have to find ways to recognise, accept and move on.

I've always had a tendency to do things quickly but as I've got older, I've learned to appreciate the value of giving myself plenty of time to learn things in detail and integrate them into my soul. I've also become aware that any attempt to avoid a feeling of powerlessness is a defence mechanism. If I reject the reality of helplessness, fragility and vulnerability, it would be false ego identification. Majnun's process has often confronted me with extreme helplessness. It took enormous trust in the divine to hang in there – to deal with whatever showed up and then move on.

Life is too short to have a festering wound inside your soul. I believe that wounds need to be healed, not by supressing them, but by recognising and integrating them. You can't waste the rest of your life feeling angry or hurt about a past event you can't change. You have to digest the experience so the healing can happen.

Majnun's healing is a long journey, and we continue to face challenges.

I believe his most recent back pain is an example of this. After the back injury, I collected a sample of Majnun's blood and sent it to a healer in our Sufi group. Her diagnosis was that his back pain was a manifestation of the tensions he still experiences when he tries to speak his truth. However, being authentic is the only way to freedom.

Be patient where you sit in the dark. The dawn is coming. Rumi

Process of inquiry – Majnun

Leyla and I use a process of inquiry to understand issues and make important decisions. It's something we've developed together quite naturally, a method of getting to the heart of the matter and understanding what is right for us. It was our inquiry that helped me understand and come to terms with the abuse I experienced. It's also inquiry we use to make decisions and prepare ourselves for new situations.

Our inquiry process is really about slow decision making and constant questioning. We patiently hold uncertainty until the uncertainty resolves itself. Together, we ask questions to get at the truth and imagine all the different options and possibilities that are out there.

Recently, we've been using our inquiry process to help us decide whether we should live together in Frankfurt, live together in Perth, or try something completely new. The only thing we're certain about is that we need to be together. Our time of living apart must end. We're spending a lot of time talking about it, thinking about the possibilities and imagining what life could be like under each option.

I've always been a person who makes decisions quickly. I like to think about the options, make a clear decision and then go for it, because my ego wants closure. If I can settle things quickly, then I don't have so much to worry about.

Leyla has taught me that a process of slow inquiry is a much more trustworthy and robust way to make decisions. I'm learning to control my need for closure and accept that things are uncertain. We don't settle on something until we're both 100 percent confident it's the best way forward.

I've learned to accept that we have conversations, imagine all the possible futures and work towards making a decision. It's learning to sit with uncertainty; a way of living that is forcing my ego to accept a bigger story, which deepens and widens my world. Sometimes I find it confronting, but it's definitely good for me.

Our process of inquiry is quite simple. We just hold the question; spend a lot of time talking about the issue and asking each other questions. Next, we explore possibilities and play make-believe, imagining what each scenario would be like; trying to picture each outcome in detail, as completely as we can. We keep asking until we are confident that we know what to do.

It takes a lot of self-discipline to hold the tension of not knowing, especially for me. I think that Leyla finds it much easier. With the tension of not knowing, things often arise that we hadn't initially thought of. We think of new possibilities and new options, and we don't always know where they came from.

Holding the tension of not knowing is the hardest part, but also the most valuable. It would be so much easier to simply take the first possibility that presented itself. But by spiralling through the process and recognising that we don't know the right decision, we're able to jointly create a much better decision.

Our process can be slow, but it's deep and thoughtful and always results in the best possible decision. I increasingly find that the tension of wondering about the decision makes me feel alive and invigorated. Many times, after we've made a decision through inquiry, we've both reflected on how positive the outcome has been and how protected we've both been by the choices we made.

Every time we imagine possible futures, we both know that everything we discuss is provisional. Nothing is set in stone until we make the final decision. We've realised that we can't know whether something is right for us until we've gone very deeply into it, through conversation and imagination. We just keep asking and asking, until we're both completely satisfied that we are making the right choice.

Here's one example of how inquiry worked successfully for us. Before I started work at the Islamic school in Perth, Leyla and I were driving from Frankfurt to Marseille in France to sort out our things. It was a long drive, and we used the time to inquire into my new job in Australia.

We asked questions and sought answers about who I would be working for, what challenges the school was facing and what issues I might be presented with. Some guidance emerged that helped us develop a very complete picture of the job I was taking. It turned out to be incredibly accurate. I walked into the new job well prepared for the issues that emerged.

Our process of inquiry is a very important part of how we live together. It gives us deep meaning and direction. It's helped us build a very strong relationship. The process helps to ensure that our individual egos are not involved too much in the decisions and provides a space where other things can come through. Obviously, our individual egos are still there, but they aren't the only voice. We let in multiple perspectives and keep asking questions until there is no longer any doubt.

When we finally land on a decision, it feels completely right. Then we always sleep on it and check again the next day whether we're both still completely confident that it's right. Only after we've slept on it do we believe it's time to move forward.

The process of inquiry has been a great learning process for me. It's taken me out of my self- absorbed capsule and helped to break me from my routine. We've built a relationship that involves deep respect, trust and imagination. We've learned to listen wholeheartedly to whatever arises from our imaginations.

Inquiry has helped me to develop my capacity to listen and flow, and my capacity to be genuinely patient. I've learned a rich patience that respects the process. It's a deep, respectful waiting until we really land on what the truth is. When we land on it, we know, because there's no more doubt.

It was inquiry that helped me get to the bottom of what was fundamentally wrong with me and supported me to go into therapy. I've learned to be patient. Inquiry has deepened the space within me where I've learned to creatively wait until we come to a decision. It's a real growth within me because I didn't used to be like this.

Our process of inquiry – Leyla

Majnun and I use an inquiry process to make important decisions. It's not for simple questions, like what colour car to buy or what to eat for dinner. It's for life-changing decisions, such as where to live or what job to accept. Most recently we've been using it to help us decide whether we should live in Perth, Frankfurt or somewhere in Turkey. Any time a decision seems complex and difficult, we use inquiry to get us there.

We've learned that the mind can be a poor advisor and logical processes don't always lead to good decisions. When we try to be only logical, we stay in the realm of ego and the result is poor. Both Majnun and I have tried rational decision-making processes, like making lists and working out all the positives and negatives. But we both believe that rational thinking doesn't help us to access deep wisdom. Our conscious minds seem to conceal the truth. We've learned from multiple bad decisions that the logical decision isn't always the best.

We've also noticed that we often face great pressure to make fast decisions. One of our most important learnings is that we mustn't give in to that pressure. Majnun and I might talk about different options for hours or days. We'll both go away and do research. We'll dig into all the various facts and possibilities, then we'll come back together and keep asking questions.

Our inquiry process developed from our decision to ride the emotional wave until we land on truth. We hold the tension of indecision and keep asking questions until we're completely confident that we've found the right decision. The decisions we reach through our inquiry process might not seem logical on the surface, and they might not make sense to other people, but they're always right for us.

We call it a process of inquiry because we acknowledge the practical, the rational and the logical, but we don't stop there. We go beyond the conscious issues and ask deeper questions. We ask questions like: What else is going on? What does our instinct say? What does our body say? What is our deeper knowledge? What would this be like? What's meant to happen? What's there for us?

We keep holding the tension of not knowing until there is absolutely no doubt about the right decision. Once we reach the decision, we feel relaxed and sure. It's like peeling an onion: you keep peeling until you get to the core.

Inquiry helps us to not be influenced by the wise decisions made by other people. We understand that what's wise for others may not be wise for us. And what's true for others might not be true for us. We've learned it's OK to listen to others, but we need to make sure their arguments don't influence our choices. The inquiry helps us stay true to ourselves.

Our inquiry process requires deep listening and equality. It comes from a deep desire to find the right path. And it needs to be the right path for us both, not a path based on one person's needs. We believe the inquiry process helps to create equality in our relationship. Our decisions are never about me getting my way or Majnun getting his way. We're interested in jointly deciding what is right for us. It creates a completely level playing field because we're both wholeheartedly committed to the process.

It was our inquiry process that helped with Majnun's recovery and helped us to keep working through the legal proceedings when things didn't seem right. Inquiry helped us realise that our lawyer wasn't working completely in Majnun's interests. The written reports didn't match what we'd discussed, and we used inquiry to gather the confidence to challenge her. Majnun was completely smashed by that pastoral meeting, and our inquiry saved his sanity. It gave us guidance how to move forward, and it gave Majnun the strength and clarity to follow through.

The inquiry process helps to dissolve any emotional or illogical attachment to an idea. It makes room for compromise between us because we're not fixed on any position. We're able to truly listen to each other and understand.

A few times we've failed to use the inquiry process and ended up making a decision that turned out to be wrong. One example was when we bought shares in oil. It had been recommended for months by some people we knew, and eventually we bought into it. The thing collapsed and we lost everything we'd invested. We were swayed by the logical advice and didn't follow our personal inquiry process.

When we make decisions through inquiry, we never make decisions that we regret. We find ourselves being thankful for or protected by the decision. Even when things don't turn out quite as expected, we still feel a deep confidence that our decision was the best one possible. Let's face it, in our lives, the unexpected is just an added bonus.

We draw on my intuition for this type of inquiry. I believe we all know a lot unconsciously, but it's hidden away. By taking the time to inquire into it, it reveals itself and helps us to be prepared. It leaves us feeling shielded as we move forward.

Objective Witness: Inquiry

It is through simple inquiry and spiritual awareness that Majnun has woken up to his experiences and taken the journey towards healing. They call it simple because the method is simple to understand. Yet the experience of living with inquiry is far from simple. It's slow and uncertain. It involves constant questioning and wondering. But when Majnun and Leyla finally land on the truth – when they're fully awake to the right decision for them – there can be no doubt. That's what inquiry offers: slow certainty, which brings peace and clarity.

There is a life in you, search that life, search the secret jewel in the mountain of your body. Rumi

Moving forward – Leyla

This book doesn't have a final chapter, because our songlines continue. All we can do here is summarise what we've discovered so far.

As you can see from our story, any form of trauma can have long-lasting effects. The resulting sense of anxiety, dissociation and depression can be debilitating. We're clearly not in a position to give therapeutic assistance or advice to people who have survived trauma. But what we can do is share with you what has supported us as we have kept walking in the hope that you can find inspiration in our words. There is every reason to be hopeful about the future.

For Majnun, regular consultations with a trauma expert made a huge difference. The trauma specialist helped him to transform painful memories into coping patterns. We both learned about EFT, the Emotional Freedom Technique, which is a form of tapping that reduces post-traumatic stress. We continue to use the technique, using an app on our phones, as often as necessary. The trauma specialist empowered us by teaching us to identify triggers and responses. He also helped me to increase my patience and accept my frustrations.

Our spiritual teacher supported us in ways we cannot begin to describe. He is a genuine spiritual teacher (and beware – there are a lot of fakes out there) and he contributed to the reversing of Majnun's soul exchange, which many survivors of sexual abuse experience.

Majnun and I witness daily the enormous benefits of our heartfelt prayers. Regular contact with a divine force that is bigger than each of us helps to reduce any sense of loneliness and sadness. We experience God as a form of calm guidance. We tune into what is present at any given moment, inquire into our experience, tease out the feelings and sensations, and land in a place that feels settled and peaceful. We call it the Land of Truth. It is a heartfelt space where the soul feels seen and God's divine guidance can flow easily.

For readers who don't subscribe to a particular faith or spiritual tradition, we recommend taking time out to meditate, engage in creative pursuits, or enjoy music. We have recently discovered an app that takes us on a short meditation journey. Its effect is noticeable for both of us: it offers deep relaxation through personalised frequencies and binaural beats. For both of us, it lowers stress and anxiety. There are many videos and apps available to assist in letting go of an over-active mind. We can recommend Michael Sealey's YouTube channel for its mindfulness meditations that help reduce the voice of the inner critic.

Trauma survivors are supported by fully inhabiting their bodies. Any physical activity or guided meditation that achieves more presence in the body and reduces the mental noise is likely to be helpful. Majnun likes to walk, while I prefer to cycle and swim. I have recently discovered the Wim Hof Method of breathing, cold therapy and commitment, and am finding it very useful for keeping myself in the present NOW.

Every person's songline is unique, and the tools that have helped us may not be appropriate for you. Our main message is that there is hope. The human soul is remarkably resilient, and there are professional resources available that can help you.

We hope this book has shown trauma survivors and their partners that there is a way forward. There's no 'one size fits all' method to trauma recovery, but if you look for it, you will find the unique size that fits you. The journey never ends, and wounds take time to heal. But the wound is the place where light enters, and we encourage you to find your light and share it with others.

Majnun and I offer workshops (both in person and online) designed to help people navigate their spiritual journeys. Our workshops cannot replace specialised sessions with trained trauma experts. However, we can accompany you while you discover and follow your personal songlines and navigate your spiritual territory. You can check out our website here: **www.instituteforspiritualawakening.com**

Anyone who enjoys travelling in new lands will marvel at the songlines we can discover within our unique souls. We are on this beautiful Planet

Earth not merely to survive, but for our soul to thrive and reveal its sparkling gems and crystals. May you blossom as you discover the precious gifts that mark your unique songline.